The Coolest People in Books: 250 Anecdotes

David Bruce

Published by David Bruce, 2022.

While every precaution has been taken in the preparation of this book, the publisher assumes no responsibility for errors or omissions, or for damages resulting from the use of the information contained herein.

THE COOLEST PEOPLE IN BOOKS: 250 ANECDOTES

First edition. September 8, 2022.

Copyright © 2022 David Bruce.

ISBN: 979-8215664933

Written by David Bruce.

Table of Contents

Dedication

Dedicated to Cliff Craft

On Sunday, 17 May 2007, my friend Cliff Craft died in Athens, Ohio. Most people probably thought of him as a homeless scavenger, but people who knew him realized that he was a generous person. He lived in low-income housing, and he frequently allowed homeless people to stay in his apartment. Because of his illnesses, including epilepsy, he lived on a monthly Social Security check and whatever money he found on his frequent walks around town, but he was generous with the money he had. Each month, he deposited his Social Security check at Hocking Valley Bank, but not all of the money ended up in his own account. According to Hocking Valley Bank branch manager Kim Sparks, for approximately two years before Mr. Craft died, he deposited some of his money each month into an account that had been set up to help a girl who had been injured in an accident. Truly, Mr. Craft's life shows that people don't need to be wealthy to do good deeds.

***

The doing of good deeds is important. As a free person, you can choose to live your life as a good person or as a bad person. To be a good person, do good deeds. To be a bad person, do bad deeds. If you do good deeds, you will become good. If you do bad deeds, you will become bad. To become the person you want to be, act as if you already are that kind of person. Each of us chooses what kind of person we will become. To become a good person, do the things a good person does. To become a bad person, do the things a bad person does. The opportunity to take action to become the kind of person you want to be is yours.

A guru had a disciple to whom he revealed a sacred mantra, along with a warning not to reveal the mantra to anyone. The disciple asked, "What will happen if I reveal the sacred mantra?" The guru replied, "Anyone to whom you reveal the sacred mantra will learn about Ultimate Goodness and will become wiser. But you will be excluded from discipleship." Immediately, the disciple ran to the marketplace and began shouting the sacred mantra to everyone there. The other disciples came to the guru and demanded that the first disciple be excluded from discipleship because he had revealed the sacred mantra. The guru smiled, agreed, and said, "Yes, you are right. He is no longer a disciple. Today, he has become a guru."

Cover Photograph for *The Coolest People in Books: 250 Anecdotes*

https://pixabay.com/photos/child-girl-book-read-reading-857021/

***

This is a short, quick, and easy read.

Anecdotes are usually short humorous stories. Sometimes they are thought-provoking or informative, not amusing.

***

Educate Yourself

Read Like A Wolf Eats

Be Excellent to Each Other

Books Then, Books Now, Books Forever

***

Do you know a language other than English? If you do, I give you permission to translate this book, copyright your translation, publish or self-publish it, and keep all the royalties for yourself. (Do give me credit, of course, for the original book.)

Chapter 1: From Alcohol to Critics

Alcohol

• At one time, newspaper reporters used to drink — a lot. During one drinking session, Paul Galloway, reporter for the *Chicago Sun-Times*, became perturbed — make that very perturbed — about something that editor Jim Hoge had perpetrated. Mr. Galloway became so perturbed that he decided to do something about his perturbation, so he went back to the *Sun-Times* offices, picked up a chair, and threw it as hard as he could at the window of Mr. Hoge's office. Big mistake. Mr. Galloway recounted later, "Something I had not foreseen was that the window was made of Plexiglas. The chair bounced back and almost hit me." Mr. Hoge was not present at the time, and he need not ever have become aware of the event, but Mr. Galloway was still perturbed, so he insisted that the City Desk log the event, although the City Desk assistant advised him, "Forget it, Paul." The next morning, Mr. Hoge was at his desk, and he perused the log, as was his custom. He also called Mr. Galloway, who now regretted having insisted that his action of the previous night be logged, into his office. Mr. Hoge said to Mr. Galloway, "So, Paul, I understand you have a problem with our interior decoration." Mr. Galloway replied, "No, sir! I find it excellent! Nothing whatsoever wrong with it! Enviable, in fact!" Mr. Galloway was a very good writer, and Mr. Hoge was a very good editor, and very good editors realize that very good writers can occasionally disagree with very good editors, and so Mr. Hoge said, "I'm relieved. Now get back to work." Another of Mr. Galloway's stories is about the time — 2 a.m. — he was standing guard in the Army. His Major sneaked up behind him and said to him, very clearly and loudly, "Sheep." Mr. Galloway was puzzled by the word, but he stood at attention and said, "Yes, sir." The major again said, very clearly and louder than before, "SHEEP!" Mr. Galloway realized that, of course, the Major must be under a great deal of pressure and therefore his mind had snapped, but he again said, "Yes, sir." The Major, clearly angry, told him, "Don't you 'yes, sir' me! Sheep! SHEEP!" Mr. Galloway said, "Would you like me to get you a sheep, sir? I will get you a sheep as soon as I'm off watch." The Major shouted, "NO! YOU'RE A MORON! I DON'T WANT A SHEEP!" Mr. Galloway asked, "What would you like, sir?" The Major shouted, "I WOULD LIKE THE GODD*MNED PASSWORD!"[1]

• Author G.K. Chesterton delivered some proofs to his editor one night. From his bag he pulled out his corrected proofs — and a bottle of port and two glasses. Unfortunately, his editor confessed that he did not drink alcohol. Shocked, Mr. Chesterton said, "Good heavens! Give me back my proofs!"[2]

Animals

• When the pet cat of Naomi, the daughter of horror writer Stephen King, was run over, she was very upset, so the family held a funeral for the cat. Mr. King's imagination began to work, and he wondered what would happen if a cat — or a human being — were to come back to life. The novel he wrote based on his speculations got its title from a sign his children had put up: "Pets Sematary."[3]

• Frequently, silence in the wilderness, whether on land or sea, is a sign of danger. Gary Paulsen, author of *Hatchet*, knows a man who survived an attack by a great white shark while he was diving. Immediately before the attack, the ocean grew silent. Today, the man says, "I should have listened to the silence. I'd still have my right leg."[4]

• Jerry Spinelli, the author of *Maniac Magee* and *Stargirl*, gets interesting letters. A boy once wrote to invite Mr. Spinelli to visit his school so he could meet the school's pet duck. One year later, the boy again wrote Mr. Spinelli to visit his school so he could meet the school's pet duck — but to hurry because the pet duck was getting old.[5]

• One author who loved his cat was Edward Lear, writer of nonsense verse. His cat was named Foss, and Mr. Lear so loved Foss that in 1881 when he had a new villa built in San Remo, Italy, he had it built exactly like the old villa that he was moving away from. That way, Foss would feel right at home.[6]

April Fools' Day

• One day in 2010, <Lulu.com>, a Web site that allows authors to self-publish their own books in various print and electronic formats, announced a new way of publishing one's work: "We recognize electronic books and the internet are a passing fad, so we are now offering the tried-and-true handwritten scroll." Of course, this announcement was made on April Fools' Day.[7]

Authors

• Karen Cushman started writing books in her middle age, and she has certainly been successful. She spent a lot of time raising a family, which included reading children's books to her daughter, Leah. When Leah started reading young-adult novels, Karen did, too, and she realized that she enjoyed this kind of reading. In 1989, at age 47, she told her husband about an idea that she had for a book, and her husband told her to write the book. (She had been talking about writing for a long time.) In a newspaper interview, she explained why she started writing when she did: "When Leah was in her last year of high school, I felt like this psychic space was opening up in my head. It's that space that was filled with, 'Does she have her lunch money? What is she doing this weekend? Who's driving?' All those questions were going out, and I had room for other questions, like 'What if there were this girl...?'" Her first book, *Catherine, Called Birdy*, was published in 1994 and was named a Newbery Honor Book. Her second book, *The Midwife's Apprentice*, was published in 1996 and won the Newbery Medal. The Newbery Medal is given to the best children's book published in the United States each year. The Newbery Honor Books are the runners'-up.[8]

• Authors sometimes have interesting experiences, possessions, and opinions. When he was a young boy, Philip Pullman, author of the *His Dark Materials* trilogy, was walking on a road when a man on a motorcycle passed him. Soon, the motorcyclist came back, stopped, and told Philip that just ahead on the road was a dead man. Then the motorcyclist left to call the proper authorities. Young Philip had to make a decision: go home by a different route or continue on and see the dead man. He continued on and saw the dead man, who was lying peacefully on the road as if he were taking a nap. Young Philip was a little disappointed in the sight. One of the places where Mr. Pullman has done his writing is a small potting shed, crowded with trash and remarkable objects, including a six-foot-long rat that was used in a Pullman theatrical adaptation of a Sherlock Holmes short story. What Mr. Pullman is most passionate about, he says, is this: "Silence. If I were a judge, and someone came to my court and was found guilty of killing their neighbors because they played loud music all day and night, I would let them go with my blessing. There is too much noise in the world, and little of it is welcome."[9]

• In the young-adult novels by Robert Cormier, the bad guys often win. For example, in his novel *The Chocolate War*, the good guy — Jerry Renault — is murdered. He isn't murdered literally, but he is beaten — physically and mentally — so badly that he totally gives up and does not believe that there is any use in trying to fight the bad guys. Mr. Cormier's bad guys are very vividly written, and one day his wife, Connie, looked up from one of his manuscripts that she had been typing and asked him, "Who are you? We've been together all these years, but sometimes I wonder." By the way, the plot of *The Chocolate War* was suggested by a real-life event in which Peter, Mr. Cormier's son, was asked to sell chocolate for his school, but he did not want to because he was busy with other activities such as schoolwork and football. In Peter's case, his parents wrote a note saying that they agreed with his decision not to sell chocolate and Peter returned the 25 boxes of chocolate to the school. Like Jerry Renault, Peter was the only student not to sell chocolate, but unlike in Jerry's case, nothing bad happened to Peter.[10]

• S.E. Hinton practically invented young-adult literature with her first novel, *The Outsiders*, which depicts teenagers with gritty realism. "S.E." are the initials for Susan Eloise, and she began the first draft of *The Outsiders* when she was 15. However, she says that no one ever believes that, so she usually says that she started the first draft when she was 16. And since her editors don't think that anyone will believe that, they often say that she started the first draft when she was 17. At any rate, her first novel was accepted for publication on a day that was important to her: the day she graduated from high school. The novel, which has sold millions of copies, made readers of many boys; she often gets letters that say, "I didn't like to read, but then I read this book."[11]

• Novelist Walter Tevis (author of *The Hustler*, *The Color of Money*, and *The Man Who Fell to Earth*) lived in many places in the United States, ending up in New York City. When people asked where he was from, he would give a different answer according to the day of the week. When asked on Tuesdays and Thursdays, he answered Kentucky. On Wednesdays and Fridays, he answered California. On the weekends, he answered Ohio. (Apparently, Mondays were a wild-card day.)[12]

• Jean Shepherd created a hoax by telling his radio listeners to go into bookstores and ask for the novel *I, Libertine* by Frederick R. Ewing — neither the novel nor the author existed. So many people asked for the novel that bookstores wanted to carry it and therefore publishers wanted to publish it. Mr. Shepherd created a synopsis of the book, and science-fiction author Theodore Sturgeon wrote the book from that synopsis. Ballantine Books published it in 1956.[13]

• In 1837, two law professors at the University of Paris waged a duel over punctuation. The disagreement was over the ending of a passage; one professor thought it should end with a semicolon, while the other professor thought it should end with a colon. According to the *Times* of London, "The one who contended that the passage in question ought to be concluded by a semicolon was wounded in the arm. His adversary maintained that it should be a colon."[14]

• Sholom Aleichem (1859-1916) was a Yiddish humorist. Among the characters he created in his stories were those that became the basis of *Fiddler on the Roof*. In 1906, he came to the United States, where he met Mark Twain, to whom he was introduced as the "Jewish Mark Twain." Mr. Twain then said that he would like to be introduced in Yiddish to Mr. Aleichem as the "American Sholom Aleichem."[15]

• A friend of science-fiction writer Philip K. Dick once read out loud a one-paragraph synopsis of Mr. Dick's novel that was the basis of the movie *Blade Runner*, then asked, "That the end of it?" Mr. Dick confirmed that it was, then joked, "Book is longer."[16]

• People identify themselves with varying degrees of honesty. One very honest person is writer Carol Schwalberg, who says that her hobbies include traveling, "visiting art galleries, and spreading malicious gossip."[17]

Autographs and Inscriptions

• J.K. Rowling sent some sample chapters of her children's book *Harry Potter and the Philosopher's Stone* to the Christopher Little Agency, which did not handle children's books. Her manuscript was rejected immediately and almost did not get read. Fortunately, a 25-year-old manuscript screener named Bryony Evens looked over the sample chapters instead of mailing them back to Ms. Rowling. She was enthusiastic about what she read, and she impressed Mr. Little with her enthusiasm, and so he asked to read the entire manuscript. The rest, as they say, is history. Ms. Evens met Ms. Rowling later, in 1998, when she waited in line for Ms. Rowling to sign a Harry Potter book. Ms. Rowling was very happy to meet her, and she signed the book in this way: "To Bryony — who is the most important person I've ever met in a signing queue & the first person ever to see merit in Harry Potter. With huge thanks. J.K. Rowling."[18]

• Sid Fleischman started out writing books for adults, but he changed the audience he wrote for because of something his older daughter, Jane, said after she had gotten an autograph by children's book author Leo Politi at the Santa Monica Public Library. Jane's mother said, "Daddy writes books, too," and Jane replied, "Yes, but no one reads his books." Very quickly, he became very successful as a writer of books for children. In his first children's book, *Mr. Mysterious and Company*, he named the child characters after his own children: Jane, Paul, and Anne. Like Mr. Politi, Mr. Fleischman signed autographs at the Santa Monica Public Library. Standing in line to get his autograph was his seven-year-old daughter, Anne. Mr. Fleischman says, "I knew I had arrived."[19]

• Ernest Hemingway once visited Robert Benchley and discovered that Mr. Benchley had a first edition of every book that Hemingway had published, including his first book, *In Our Time*. He said, "So you were going to save this, and then sell it when it got to be worth a lot of money — all right, I'll fix you." He then wrote a filthy inscription in the book. Next he took Mr. Benchley's copy of *A Farewell to Arms* and filled in the original dirty dialogue that the publisher had not seen fit to print and had represented by blanks. On its flyleaf, he wrote, "Corrected edition with filled-in blanks. Very valuable — sell quick."[20]

• William Faulkner once stayed for a few days at the New York apartment of writers Frank Sullivan and Corey Ford. When he left, he took a copy of *The Sound and the Fury* from Mr. Ford's bookshelf, then inscribed it, "Corey Ford's book is hereby presented to Frank Sullivan with the regards of Wm. Faulkner." Mr. Sullivan declined to return the book to Mr. Ford.[21]

• On June 26, 1997, J.K. Rowling's first book, *Harry Potter and the Philosopher's Stone*, was published in the United Kingdom. She went to a bookstore to see her book, and she was tempted to sign all the copies, but she decided not to in case she got in trouble.[22]

• Because he was so famous, humorous poet Ogden Nash was frequently asked to give his autograph. This didn't bother him, except when young autograph hounds thrust a piece of paper and a pen at him and said, "Who are you? Sign here!"[23]

Books

• Some writers are incredibly prolific. At age 73 in 2008, science-fiction writer Robert Silverberg had written approximately 300 novels, 600 short works of fiction, and 100 nonfiction books. Is that all, you ask? No. He has edited approximately 100 anthologies. (Let's not mention all the Forewords and Introductions and other miscellaneous writings.) He writes so much that he has used more than 50 pseudonyms to keep from overwhelming readers. Of course, once in a while people ask him how he writes that much. He replies, "One word at a time." As you would expect, he has many anecdotes about his years of writing. For example, when he was still a college student, a professional science-fiction writer named Randall Garrett moved into the apartment next door. Mr. Silverberg had already started writing and publishing science fiction, and Mr. Garrett told him, "I'm a professional writer with a lot of experience. I think we could work together. You are very disciplined; I am not." Mr. Silverberg says, "It worked out beautifully for two or three years. When he would fall asleep at his typewriter because he'd been up all night drinking, I would pick up the manuscript and continue writing. Eventually I got married, and my wife said, 'That man is not going to enter this house.'" By the way, a good writer nearing the end of his life ought to be able to think up a good epitaph, right? Right. Mr. Silverberg says, "A few years ago, I actually did come up with a mocking sort of epitaph for myself. It's this: 'Here lies Robert Silverberg. He spent most of his life in the future. Now he's in the past.'"[24]

• In 2008, Paul Constant, book critic for the Seattle newspaper *The Stranger*, attended BookExpo America (BEA), the annual book-industry convention. One thing he noticed was what he called "unscrupulous booksellers" who grabbed as many free advance reader's copies as possible so that they could later sell them online — illegally.

Of course, the publishers are aware that unscrupulous booksellers do this, and so they have a rule against bringing rolling luggage carts to the convention because the carts can be filled with many, many free advance reader's copies. However, Mr. Constant writes that "some demented booksellers find ways around that: One woman wheels into the hall in a wheelchair and then stands up and wheels the empty chair around to stack books in the seat like a wheelbarrow."[25]

• Novelist Leif Enger got the writing bug from Lin, his brother, a writer of short stories whose first solo-written novel is *Undiscovered Country*, a retelling of Shakespeare's *Hamlet*, but set in Minnesota. Their father read Lin's novel, then watched Mel Gibson's movie version of *Hamlet*. The father, who may be a little biased, says, "I think Lin's a little better than Shakespeare." Leif has written a Western titled *So Brave, Young, and Handsome*, for which he did research on the history of the Hundred and One ranch. Among other things, the managers had brought in Geronimo, who was then old, and had him shoot a buffalo. Leif says, "They billed it as 'Geronimo's Last Buffalo.' Nobody knew it was really his first buffalo because the Apache didn't hunt buffalo."[26]

• While in France, William Donaldson bought a pornographic novel and started reading it in public, first taking the precaution of putting a different book jacket on the novel. The book jacket was for a compilation of essays against the A-bomb, including essays by Bertrand Russell, Philip Toynbee, and other intellectuals. Peter Ustinov happened to be walking by, and seeing the book jacket, he asked Mr. Donaldson if he could look at the book. Mr. Donaldson readily gave him permission and handed the book to him. Mr. Ustinov read one filthy paragraph, and then looked at the book jacket. Then he read another filthy paragraph and again looked at the book jacket. Finally, speechless for once in his life, he handed the book back to Mr. Donaldson and exited.[27]

• When Gary Paulsen was 14 years old, he felt cold on the street and so he went into a public library to warm up. The librarian gave him a library card and checked out a book for him. It took him a month to read that book, but soon each week he was reading two or three books. Mr. Paulsen says, "She saved me, she really did, by giving me that book. She turned me into a reader, made me love reading and books and stories." As an adult, Mr. Paulsen has written over 100 books, including the very popular book *Hatchet*, starring a boy named Brian who has to survive alone in the Canadian wilderness with only a hatchet and the clothing he is wearing.[28]

• Like so many of us, Brazilian author Paulo Coelho owned too many books. He put them on shelves, and when he returned home one day, he discovered that the shelves had collapsed. Reflecting that if he had been home he might have crushed to death by the books and shelves, he decided to greatly reduce the number of books he owned — to 400, which he says is still a high number if he intends to reread all those books.[29]

• When she died, Agatha Christie left behind two gifts for the fans of her detective characters Hercule Poirot and Jane Marple — two mystery books. *Curtain* told about M. Poirot's final case, and *Sleeping Murder* told about Miss Marple's final case. Ms. Christie dedicated the mysteries to her daughter and her husband. After writing the mysteries in 1940, she left them in a vault to which only her husband had access. As Ms. Christie wished, the two mysteries were not published until after her death.[30]

Children

• In 2008, author Barbara Kingsolver's younger daughter, Lily, was 11 years old. According to Ms. Kingsolver, "The wisdom of each generation is necessarily new. This tends to dawn on us in revelatory moments, brought to us by our children." As an example, she brings up her daughter, whom she walks to the school bus stop and talks to until the bus arrives. This is a good time, but a few weeks previously, Lily looked her over and then told her, "Mom, just so you know, the only reason I'm letting you wear that outfit is because of your age."

When the bus arrived, Ms. Kingsolver hid behind a building. That is an example of new knowledge. In Ms. Kingsolver's words, "It's okay [...] to deck out and turn up as the village idiot" when you are old enough. What about the old knowledge? Ms. Kingsolver says, "Honestly, it is harrowing for me to try to teach 20-year-old students, who earnestly want to improve their writing. The best I can think to tell them is this: Quit smoking, and observe posted speed limits. This will improve your odds of getting old enough to be wise." According to Ms. Kingsolver, the books that are good are the books that are wise.[31]

• Kathy Lette is an Australian author who says, "All I do in my books is write down the way women talk when there are no men around." She lives with a human-rights lawyer with whom she has had children. Unfortunately, this means that she changes lots of diapers. According to Ms. Lette, this has an effect on her writing, just as having children has an effect on every female author: "For every baby she has, a female author loses out on writing about three books." She has asked Geoffrey, the human-rights lawyer she lives with, to change diapers (nappies), but the first time she asked, he replied, "But I've got 250 people on death row in Trinidad." She jokes that she did not say anything then, but "after another 4,000 nappies, I replied, 'Oh, let them die.' After the second baby, I was like, 'I'm going to go there and kill them myself. Human rights begin at home!'"[32]

• George Orwell (the author of *Animal Farm* and *1984*) and his wife, Eileen, adopted a three-week-old boy in June of 1944. Mr. Orwell's real name was Eric Blair, so they named the boy Richard Horatio Blair. After his wife died, Mr. Orwell raised the boy on the island of Jura so he would be away from the city. There, Mr. Orwell let the boy learn from his mistakes. For example, young Richard found a tobacco pipe in the garden and filled it with cigarette butts that he took from the fireplace. Mr. Orwell saw him do this, and he handed young Richard his lighter. In a letter, Mr. Orwell reported on the result of young Richard's attempt at smoking: "I'm sorry to say that Richard took to smoking recently, but he made himself horribly sick and that has put him off it."[33]

• Karen Hesse, Newbery Award-winning author of *Out of the Dust*, was a sickly and whiny child. Her mother even gave her gold stars on the days that Karen did not cry, but Karen earned very few gold stars. Still, Karen was eager to try new things. At around age eight, she tried to fly, launching herself into space from the top of some stairs leading to the second floor of her house. She made it almost all the way down the stairs before hitting the floor. Encouraged by this seeming success, she wanted to try flying out of a second-floor window, but fortunately a neighbor saw her sitting on the window ledge. The neighbor telephoned Karen's mother, who stopped the flying attempt.[34]

• Children are interested in and remember the details of exciting stories. For example, J.R.R. Tolkien used to tell the stories that eventually became his fantasy novel *The Hobbit* to his young son, Christopher, who would listen to a story, then say, "Last time, you said Bilbo's front door was blue, and you said Thorin had a silver tassel on his hood, but you've just said that Bilbo's front door was green, and the tassel on Thorin's hood was gold." When this happened, Mr. Tolkien would say, "D*mn the boy," but he would also take notes on what Christopher had said so that he could make the stories consistent.[35]

• When author George Plimpton was a kid, he admired New York Giants' ace pitcher Carl Hubbell, who had thrown so many screwballs that he was deformed — his palm turned to the outside. Young George used to walk with his palm turned to the outside, hoping that people would think that he threw screwballs, but his father made him stop. Mr. Plimpton says, "He said it looked as if I had tumbled out a window and my parents didn't have enough money to set the broken arm properly.[36]

• When Fay Kanin was about 12 years old, she discovered that people could get paid for writing. A newspaper called the *Elmira Star*

Gazette paid $1 for anecdotes about readers' most embarrassing moments. One dollar was a lot of money back then, so Fay invented a most embarrassing moment, wrote it up, and earned $1. She then asked a friend if she could use her name, and she earned another dollar. A little later, all three most embarrassing moments in the newspaper column were ghostwritten by Fay.[37]

• Katherine Anne Porter, author of *Ship of Fools*, started writing early. When she was six years old, she wrote a "novel," which she titled *A Nobbel — The Hermit of Halifax Cave*.[38]

• James Russell Lowell once saw a building with this sign in front: "Home for Incurable Children." He pointed out the sign to a friend, then said, "They'll get me in there some day."[39]

Clothing

• Thomas Butts once called on Mr. and Mrs. William Blake, only to find that they were sitting naked in a summerhouse. Nudity didn't bother either of the Blakes, so Mr. Blake called to Mr. Butts, "Come in. It's only Adam and Eve, you know."[40]

• When Gary Paulsen, the popular children's author of *Hatchet*, speaks before groups of young readers, he often wears a cap that bears the message, "Read Like a Wolf Eats."[41]

Critics

• In his old age, author Gore Vidal moved from his villa (La Rondinaia) in Italy back to the United States because his being in a wheelchair made it impossible for him to live in the Italian villa, situated as it was on a cliff. In his United States abode is a set of chairs, which he bought in Rome from a dealer who tried to convince him that the chairs were created for a maharaja. Mr. Vidal told the dealer, "No, they're not. They come from the set of the movie *Ben-Hur*. I wrote it." Mr. Vidal is one of the uncredited writers of the movie, and he claims to have been forced to write for the movies and popular culture because *The New York Times* had started to ignore him as a writer of books. He says, "If you didn't appear in the daily *New York Times*, you were non-existent. Every other journal, including *Time* and *Newsweek*, followed its lead. And that is what drove me into television, Broadway, and the movies." Mr. Vidal found a way to get close to even with *The New York Times*. He wrote three mystery novels using the pseudonym Edgar Box. These mysteries, he says, "were glowingly reviewed in the *Times*."[42]

• The Australian novelist Shirley Hazzard is highly rated by critics, yet little known by readers. In addition to writing novels, she also has memorized much, much poetry. In fact, her knowledge of poetry led to her and her husband, Flaubert scholar Francis Steegmuller, meeting the novelist Graham Greene. In a restaurant at Capri, they overheard him trying to remember a line of poetry. Ms. Hazzard knew the line and recited it, and the three became friends. Critics do appreciate her. At the end of an interview with Ms. Hazzard, journalist Bryan Appleyard told her, "Thank you. You have written some beautiful novels." She replied, "Pardon, what did you say?" Mr. Appleyard repeated his statement, and she admitted, "I heard you. I just wanted to hear you say it again."[43]

• People do make mistakes. While Kurt Vonnegut, Jr., author of *Slaughterhouse-Five*, was on a panel at City College, a woman asked him this question: "Why did you put exactly one hundred 'So it goes's' in *Slaughterhouse-Five*?" Mr. Vonnegut replied that he was not aware that he had used that exact number. Also on the panel was critic John Simon, who disappeared while everyone had coffee, and then reappeared and said to Mr. Vonnegut, "One hundred and three." Some critics have been very happy to place Mr. Vonnegut in a category in which he may or may not belong. At a party, he was introduced to cultural commissar Jason Epstein, who thought for a moment, said "Science fiction," and then walked away. Mr. Vonnegut says, "He just had to place me, that's all."[44]

• Occasionally, novelist Kurt Vonnegut, Jr., taught creative writing, and of course he critiqued the writing of other people. A Smith undergraduate asked him to critique a short story that she described as "a heartwarming account" of the death of her grandmother. Despite its frequent humor, Mr. Vonnegut's work is often dark, and he thought that the short story was "too gushy" and therefore suggested, "Have you ever thought about making your grandmother insane?" Most likely, the Smith undergraduate was made uncomfortable by the suggestion, just as Mr. Vonnegut felt uncomfortable because of a comment that was made after he told someone that the name "Vonnegut" was German: "Germans killed six million of my cousins." (Of course, during World War II Mr. Vonnegut fought on the side of the Allies.)[45]

• Jessica Morgan and Heather Cocks write a blog called GoFugYourself in which they criticize celebrities who demonstrate poor fashion sense. In 2008 they came out with a book titled *Go Fug Yourself Presents: The Fug Awards*. Of course, their experiences are interesting, and they have learned from them. Ms. Morgan says, "I have learned that people who write hate mail tend to have considerably worse spelling and grammar than people who write non-hate mail." So what is in the future for the celebrity-criticizing duo? Ms. Cocks says, "I would like to say the future looks like a closet full of Louboutin shoes and designer dresses, but I keep forgetting to buy lottery tickets, so I'm guessing that will never come to pass."[46]

• World-class author Isaac Bashevis Singer once read a story in front of a group of 12 Jews who were too poor to pay him anything. After he had read the story, a man stood up and said that the story was not a good story because it was not a Zionist story. Therefore, the man said, "I spit on your story." Each of the other members of the audience stood up in turn and said that the story was not good for various reasons, and each of them said that they spit on the story. One man even said he spit on the story twice — once because it was not Orthodox, and once because it was not Zionist. So, Mr. Singer said, "From 12 people I collected 13 spits."[47]

• Readers can impact an author. Kurt Vonnegut, Jr., wrote an ending for his novel *Breakfast of Champions* and sent it to his publisher. He lived near his publisher and a lot of mail and messages went back and forth, and a couple of young employees in the production department met him and told him that they didn't like the ending: "That's not the way we thought it should end." Mr. Vonnegut thanked them, looked at the ending, realized that they were right, and wrote another ending — the one that appeared in the published book.[48]

• The person who discovered author Anita Loos in England and helped make her comic novel *Gentlemen Prefer Blondes* popular there was poet A.E. Housman. He read the novel, then told all his friends and fellow professors at Cambridge University about it. Soon everyone in Cambridge was reading it and thereafter the novel became popular throughout England.[49]

Chapter 2: From Death to Gays and Lesbians

Death

• Some people find unusual ways to die. William S. Burroughs, author of *Naked Lunch*, married a woman to help her escape from the Nazis. She worked for a playwright named Ernst Toller, and she always returned promptly from lunch at 1 p.m. However, one day she met and spoke to a fellow refugee she knew and so she arrived back from lunch 10 minutes late and discovered that Mr. Toller had hung himself. It turned out that he had attempted suicide at other times, but he had always been careful to do so at a time and place where he knew that someone would rescue him. Because Mrs. Burroughs arrived 10 minutes late from her lunch, he succeeded this time in killing himself. OK, that is morbid, but this is cool (and it's about life): Mr. Burroughs is well aware that children find it easy to pick up languages. When he was living in Mexico, he would speak to a shopkeeper, who would then ask Mr. Burroughs' four-year-old son, "What did he say?" And his four-year-old son would tell the shopkeeper, in Spanish, what his father had said.[50]

• Studs Terkel remembers that when he met his wife, Ida, she was wearing a maroon dress. He also remembers that she made a lot more money than he did: "It was like dating a CEO. I borrowed 20 bucks from her for our first date. I never paid her back." Unfortunately for Studs, his wife died first: "She was seven days older than me, and I would always joke that I married an older woman. That's the thing: Who's gonna laugh at my jokes? At those jokes I've told a million times? [...] Who's gonna be there to laugh?" When Studs died, he had planned for his cremated ashes to be mixed with his wife's ashes and then to be scattered on Bughouse Square, a park. He said, laughing, "Scatter us there. It's against the law. Let 'em sue us."[51]

• After John F. Kennedy was assassinated on November 22, 1963, 11-year-old Karen Hess, a future author of young readers' books, watched his funeral on television. She was so affected by the assassination and funeral that she started folding everything — towels, clothing, etc. — into a tight triangle like the American flag that was given to President Kennedy's widow, Jackie.[52]

Editors

• Cynthia Ozick labored long over her first first novel, writing 300,000 words over seven years before abandoning the too-ambitious project. She then labored long over her second first novel, writing more than 800 pages over seven years before sending it to an editor who marked the first 100 pages before sending it back to her with this note: "If you do everything my red pencil suggests, and of course there will be more in this vein, we will accept your novel for publication. But if you decline to follow my red pencil's indispensable advice, then we will decline to publish." Ms. Ozick declined to make the changes and she says that she sent back this note: "Seven years have I labored for these words, and yet another seven years; so I say unto you, Nay, not one jot or tittle will I alter or undo." To which the editor — she calls him "blessed editor" — responded, "OK, we'll take it anyway." Good choice. Ms. Ozick outlived the editor by decades, but he accepted her first novel that was published, and in 2008 she won the 2008 PEN/ Nabokov Lifetime Achievement Award.[53]

• Comic writer Robert Benchley was frequently late in delivering his writing, but he always took the time to make up some excuse for why it was late. Once, he used the excuse that his mother was ill and he had to leave town to stay with her. Unfortunately, Art Shields, the editor of *Harper's Bazaar*, found out that Mr. Benchley was still in town. Mr. Benchley then swung into action, sending telegrams to his friends around the country and asking them to send telegrams in his name to Mr. Shields. Telegrams arrived saying that Mr. Benchley was in Hollywood making a movie with Greta Garbo, in Sante Fe becoming a member of the Navajo Indian tribe, in Maine working as a guide for a group of hunters, etc. Eventually, Mr. Shields sent Mr. Benchley a telegram: "I GATHER YOU HAVEN'T DONE THE PIECE."[54]

• As editor of the *Emporia Gazette*, William Allen White read and rejected many stories. A woman wrote him after one of her stories was rejected, "You sent back last week a story of mine. I know that you did not read the story, for as a test I pasted together pages 18, 19, and 20. The story came back with these pages still pasted. So I know that you are a fraud and turn down stories without reading them." Mr. White wrote her in reply, "At breakfast when I open an egg I don't have to eat it all to determine if it is bad."[55]

Education

• In 2006 novelist Ian McEwan, author of *Atonement*, weeded his fiction library in his London town house. Then he and his younger son, Greg, gave away 30 novels in a nearby park. Mr. McEwan says that "every young woman we approached ... was eager and grateful to take a book." However, the men responded with "Nah, nah. Not for me. Thanks, mate, but no." Mr. McEwan concludes, "When women stop reading, the novel will be dead." By the way, Mr. McEwan's younger son, Greg, had to study Mr. McEwan's novel *Enduring Love* that featured two characters named Clarissa and Joe and answer this question: What is the moral center of the book? Greg asked his father about the novel, and Mr. McEwan said, "Well, I think Clarissa's got everything wrong." Greg wrote an essay in which he stated that, and his teacher gave him a D. Mr. McEwan says, "The teacher didn't care what I thought. She thought that Joe was too 'male' in his thinking. Well. I mean, I only wrote the damn thing ." In addition, Mr. McEwan's older son, Ian, Jr., remembers, "I once had to answer a question on Dad's book *Enduring Love* for my A-level English. I based the answer on what he told me while writing it. I got a low B."[56]

• When he was a child, Walter Dean Myers loved comic books, even smuggling the forbidden reading into his house in the legs of his pants. When he was in the 5th grade, his teacher caught him reading a comic book in class. Disgusted, she handed him a book of Scandinavian fairy tales and said, "If you're going to sit here and read, you might as well read something worthwhile." Mr. Myers remembers, "It was the best thing that ever happened to me." He read that book and other books she handed to him, and he became a reader. He worried that reading might not be well regarded by many of his friends, and often he carried library books inside a brown paper bag so that other children could not see them. His teacher, Mrs. Conway, helped him in other ways. Young Walter had a speech impediment, and she required students to recite a poem out loud in front of the class; however, the poem could be something that the student had written. Walter wrote a poem that used only words that he could pronounce well, and he impressed the other students with his recitation.[57]

• Hunter S. Thompson worked very hard to become a writer. He wrote lots of stuff on his own, of course, but he also would type pages of material by F. Scott Fitzgerald and Ernest Hemingway simply to "feel the rhythm" of the way they wrote. This hard work paid off when he wrote his breakthrough book, *Hell's Angels*, at age 29. The first part was more scholarly than the second, which was much more "gonzo" — the kind of writing associated with Mr. Thompson, who discovered that he had only four days to write the second part. He simply holed himself up in a room with what he considered the necessities of life — Wild Turkey and Dexedrine — and created the second half of the book. By the way, Mr. Thompson says that he was able to do this not because of the alcohol and the drug, but because of the 15 years that he had spent learning to write.[58]

• Young-people's author Richard Peck taught for a while, but he quit because he thought that educational standards and the quality of students dropped dramatically during the 1960s. Even the brightest students were not so bright — or if they were bright, their brightness was dimmed by excessive pride. Anthropologist Margaret Mead once lectured some gifted girls at Hunter College High School, where he taught. She suggested that the girls learn real-world skills such as secretarial skills or nursing skills since such skills are useful in life — in addition to the academic work that the girls were doing. One of the students replied, "Lady, I don't think you know who we are. We aren't going to be secretaries. We're gifted!" Mr. Peck does have strong opinions. For example, he says, "Watching television is what you do with your life when you don't want to live it."[59]

• Haki R. Madhubuti came from a home that did not seem to be a breeding ground for success. His mother had a cleaning job that required her to sleep with the building owner. Later, she became a drunkard and then an addict to hard drugs and finally a prostitute to pay for the hard drugs. Mr. Madhubuti says about growing up, "Poetry in my home was almost as strange as money." He avoided any bad effects of his upbringing because his mother sent him to the library to borrow and read *Black Boy*, a novel by Richard Wright. At first, he resisted because he didn't to want to go up to a white librarian and request any book with the word "black" in the title. However, when he realized how important the book was to his mother, he borrowed the book and read it to please her. That book got him hooked on reading, and he became a prominent African-American poet.[60]

• Louisa May Alcott, author of *Little Women*, grew up in a poor but ethical family. Her mother taught her to live by these rules: "1. Rule yourself. 2. Love your neighbor. 3. Hope, and keep busy." On her fourth birthday, young Louisa passed out servings of plum cake to the guests at her party. Unfortunately, the little guests outnumbered the servings of plum cake, and someone would have to go without. Since it was her birthday, Louisa wanted plum cake, even though one of the little guests would go without, but her mother told her, "I know my Lou will not let the little friend go without." Louisa did give the plum cake to her friend, and her mother rewarded her with a kiss. Louisa called this incident her "first lesson in the sweetness of self-denial."[61]

• Jonathan Swift had a bad habit of not tipping. Once, a boy delivered a package to Dean Swift. Because he knew that he would not receive a tip, the delivery boy's manners were abrupt. Dean Swift told the boy that he needed to learn some manners, and so for educational purposes he told the boy to pretend to be Dean Swift while he pretended to be the delivery boy. Dean Swift then said, "Sir, Mr. Brown has sent you this package of fruit and begs you to accept it." The delivery boy said, "Tell Mr. Brown that I accept the package with great thanks, and here's half a crown for yourself." Having learned his lesson, Dean Swift smiled, then gave the delivery boy half a crown.[62]

• Children's author Jane Yolen began reading and writing at an early age — and kept right on going. In the first grade, she read overnight a book that the students were supposed to read for an entire semester, so the teacher moved her up to the second grade, where she wrote the words and music to the class play. The play featured vegetables, and in the big finale they came together and formed a salad. While attending Smith College, she wrote in verse a final exam essay about American intellectual history — and got an A! And on her 22nd birthday, she sold her first real book.[63]

• Young-people's author Richard Peck had a tough English teacher named Miss Franklin during his senior year in high school. On the students' first day of class, she announced, "I can get all of you in this room into the colleges of your choice — or I can keep you out." When he handed in his first composition in her course, she wrote on it, "Never express yourself again on my time. Find a more interesting topic." Seventeen-year-old Richard asked her what would be a more interesting topic than himself. She replied, "Almost anything."[64]

• A friend of young-people's author William Sleator was a very good student and wrote very good papers. In fact, one paper was so good that a teacher new to the school gave her an F because he thought it was plagiarized. She did not protest, but after the teacher gave an in-class writing assignment and read her paper, which was excellent and which the teacher knew could not have been plagiarized, the teacher apologized to the student and raised the F he had previously given her to an A.[65]

• Flannery O'Connor used to take castor-oil sandwiches to the St. Vincent's Grammar School for Girls she attended in Savannah, Georgia. Why? She didn't want to share her lunch with the other students. Later, she attended the Peabody School in Milledgeville, where she was required to sew a set of clothing for her Home Economics class. On examination day, she brought her pet duckling and the set of clothing she had made to school. The set of clothing consisted of underwear and outerwear — all created to fit the duck.[66]

• Milton Friedman was a Nobel Prize-winning economist who served as an economic adviser to Israeli Prime Minister Menachem Begin. After Mr. Friedman had given a speech, Shlomo Lorincz asked him, "In the Talmud, Hillel summarized Judaism in one sentence: 'What is hateful to you, do not do to your neighbor: this is the whole Torah. The rest is commentary.' Could you summarize economics in one sentence?" Mr. Friedman replied, "Yes — there is no such thing as a free lunch."[67]

• Lynne Reid Banks, author of *The Indian in the Cupboard*, taught English for nine years in Israel. She once attended a reading conference where she spoke in front of a group of children who had plastic bags filled with reading materials. The children grew restless and started rustling the bags, and to get their attention, she kicked the bag out from underneath a boy. Another teacher wrote her an angry letter protesting her action, but the boy invited Ms. Banks to join his soccer team.[68]

• M.E. Kerr, author of books for young people, sometimes gives presentations in classrooms. One teacher who gave a questionnaire to students following Ms. Kerr's presentation shared one with her. One question was this: "What did you like most about Ms. Kerr's talk?" A student named Wallace had answered, "Sitting next to Brenda." By the way, Ms. Kerr's real name is Marijane Agnes Meaker. The pseudonym "M.E. Kerr" is a play on the name "Meaker."[69]

• Many people who tell stories have the bad habit of stopping repeatedly to ask the listener if he or she has heard the story before. Henry Irving was one such person. In telling a story to Mark Twain, he stopped three different times to ask if Mr. Twain had heard the story before. Finally, Mr. Twain could stand it no longer and said, "I can lie once, I can lie twice for the sake of politeness, but there I draw the line. I not only heard the story — I invented it."[70]

• David Foster Wallace's mother was an English teacher at a community college. She had an interesting way of teaching David and Amy, his sister, proper grammar. If either of them made an error in usage during conversation at the supper table, she would pretend to have a coughing fit until the child acknowledged his or her error and corrected it.[71]

• Countee Cullen took his poetry seriously — and his teaching. In Paris, he once met a student to whom he had given a failing grade in French. The student thanked him for the failing grade because after he had received it, he had studied French seriously and the French government had hired him as a translator.[72]

Fame

• For many years, Alistair Cooke lived in the United States and was famous in Great Britain because of his BBC radio program *Letter from America* and his articles in *The Guardian*. However, Susan, his own daughter, did not know that her father was famous. She found out when her family went to London on vacation, and the British maître d' in a restaurant made a huge fuss over the recently knighted Sir Alistair Cooke. She was shocked, went into the ladies' room, and thought, "What the heck!" Of course, Sir Alistair knew he was famous, and he learned how to deal with it. Sometimes someone would recognize him and say, "Aren't you ...?" He always replied, "That's right. I'm Bob Hope." One day, he said that to a woman, and the woman replied,

"Isn't that interesting? I'm Mrs. Bob Hope." (She really was, and they both laughed.) By the way, Sir Alistair had high standards for language, both written and spoken. He seriously disliked for his daughters to say "um," and Emma's sister's habit of saying "you know" drove him to yell, "I don't know, I don't know! That's why you're talking and I'm not, because you're going to tell me something I don't know!"[73]

• Neil Gaiman, author of *Coraline*, an excellent book that was made into an excellent movie, is like a rock star. His film agent, Jon Levin, discovered how popular Mr. Gaiman was when they went to a meeting at Warner Brothers. All of the secretaries asked Mr. Gaiman for his autograph, and someone pointed out, "That never happens when Tom Cruise is here." Mr. Gaiman is a true original. He proposed to his girlfriend, Amanda Palmer of the punk group the Dresden Dolls, by using a Sharpie to draw a ring on her finger.[74]

• Gabriel García Marquez became famous for his novel *One Hundred Years of Solitude*, which told the story of the Columbian village Macondo. *New York Times* book critic John Leonard read the novel, then wrote, "The great American novel has been written by a Latin American." And in the early 1970s, when Mr. Marquez visited Cuba, some peasants asked him what he did for a living. He replied that he had written a book titled *Cien años de soledad*. The peasants cried, "Macondo!"[75]

Family

• Much of John Cheever's life was dark, including the time after he was conceived but had not yet been born. After all, when his father learned that his mother was pregnant with John, he invited the local abortion doctor over for dinner — his way of expressing his opinion of the pregnancy. Mr. Cheever, a homosexual, was married for 40-some years to Mary Winternitz, who once told him after he had spent several days in a hospital, "[I]t was nice while you were away to have a dry toilet seat." (Mr. Cheever used this line in his novel *Falconer*.)[76]

• Max Beerbohm was the younger brother of the famous actor Herbert Beerbohm Tree. Max once announced that he was going to write a series of articles about the brothers of famous men. When someone asked whether Max was brother to Mr. Tree, Max acknowledged the relationship, then added, "He is coming into the series."[77]

Fans

• Harlan Ellison is aware that some fans can treat those they adore — or sometimes adore and sometimes hate — very, very badly. In fact, he once wrote an article on this subject after doing research: He contacted 100 writers to ask, "What's the worst thing fans ever did to you?" Mr. Ellison received many answers about worst things, "Not the least of which is somebody walking up to Alan Dean Foster in a corridor at a science-fiction convention and throwing a cup of warm vomit on him for no reason."[78]

• Author Terry McMillan has a good response when people tell her, "Hey, you look just like Terry McMillan." She says, "I get that a lot, and I resent it. Terry McMillan is much older."[79]

Fathers

• To a large extent Charles Bukowski's public image is that of a dirty old man, and to a large extent the public image is the truth. However, Mr. Bukowski can surprise people. For example, even though much of his home was sloppy — visitors noticed many, many empty tubes of Preparation H among the litter in his bathroom — he kept his desk orderly and professional, in contrast to the mess surrounding it. Clearly, writing was one area of Mr. Bukowski's life that mattered to him. He took writing seriously, as is evidenced by the mass quantities of writing that he produced. In addition, his relationships with women could be sensitive. The first woman he had more than a passing sexual relationship with was an alcoholic barfly. She eventually was taken in an ambulance to the Los Angeles County Hospital because of excessive alcohol consumption, where doctors discovered that she had cancer in an advanced stage as well as cirrhosis of the liver. When she awoke out of a comatose state, she saw Mr. Bukowski by her hospital bed and said to him, "I knew it would be you." Shortly afterward, she died. He wrote this elegy for her: "For Jane, With All the Love I Had, Which Was Not Enough." And his letters to his daughter, Marina, show a parental concern, as when he wrote, "PLEASE BE VERY CAREFUL WHEN YOU CROSS THE STREET. LOOK *BOTH* WAYS." For her, he wrote "Love Poem to Marina."[80]

• The father of Richard Restak, M.D., helped educate him when Richard was a child. He told young Richard that occasionally he would place a dollar in the front flap of the book cover of the family's dictionary. He would not do this every day, but he would do it once in a while. He also told Richard that he should open the dictionary and learn a new word every day; after all, Richard would not know on which day his father would put a dollar in the dictionary. Whether Richard earned a dollar or not, he would be rewarded. His father told him, "Every day a new word will be your reward, and on some days you will be doubly rewarded." Richard kept up the habit of learning a word a day throughout his life and has written books about the brain.[81]

• Kurt Vonnegut, Jr., worked hard to be a good writer, but for a long time influential critics who did not like science fiction regarded him "merely" as a writer of science fiction. Eventually, and especially with the publication of *Slaughterhouse-Five*, he became famous. Mark, his son, who was named after Mark Twain, was once asked what it was like to grow up with a famous father. He replied, "When I was growing up, my father was a car salesman who couldn't get a job teaching at Cape Cod Junior College."[82]

• The father of philosopher George Santayana was a frugal man. When George was a child, he asked his father why he always traveled third class. His father replied, "There is no fourth class."[83]

Food

• Philip Pullman, author of the *His Dark Materials* trilogy, is a wonderful storyteller — not just when he writes his novels, but also when he tells out loud the stories of classic literature. For example, when he and his family were on vacation, Tom, his young son, found it difficult to stay still while they waited for their food in a restaurant. Therefore, Mr. Pullman started telling him the story of Odysseus, hero of Homer's *Odyssey*, who spent 10 years at Troy in the Trojan War, and who spent another 10 years returning back home to his home island, Ithaca. Although Odysseus was the King of Ithaca, he returned home without any of his men or ships. Ever cautious, he disguised himself as a beggar, and then he set out to see if he had any friends left on the island. He found that a gang of young men who thought he was dead had had taken over his palace. They wanted to kill his son and to force his wife, Penelope, to choose one of them to marry. Eventually, Mr. Pullman reached the point in the story where Odysseus gets his great bow in his hands and strings the bow. After stringing the bow, he plucks the string on the bow just like a harp player plucks a string on a harp. Immediately, the suitors besieging Penelope feel dread because they know that Odysseus is going to try to kill all of them. At this point, Tom, who was holding a drink in his hands, was so excited that he bit a chunk out of his glass. Their waitress saw him do that, and she was so shocked that she dropped the tray with all their food on the floor. Mr. Pullman ends his story by writing, "And I sent up a silent prayer of thanks to Homer."[84]

• In December 2009, Alexandra Shulman, the editor of *Vogue* in England, weighed about 10 pounds more than she wanted to, although this was not anything that she was really concerned about. However, excess weight is something that her father was prone to, and when she was young, he worried that she might become so chunky that she would find it difficult to find a husband. (In 2009 she was divorced and had a child.) When she was attending St Paul's Girls' school, the headmistress announced publicly (all of Alexandra's schoolmates heard the headmistress), "Alexandra Shulman's mother has said she is not to have potatoes." When her father was seriously ill and in the intensive ward, she visited him, and he called out to her in a very robust voice, "God, Alexandra, you've put on weight." She immediately thought, "OK, he isn't going to die yet."[85]

• As an author who writes frequently about survival in the wilderness, Gary Paulsen has eaten some strange meals. In a village along the Bering Sea, he came across a six-year-old boy who was sucking blood from a hole in the carcass of a seal. The boy asked Mr. Paulsen, "Want some?" As an inquisitive author, Mr. Paulsen did — and he says that the taste was "not unpleasant." Later, he saw the boy eating Crisco straight from the can, dipping his fingers into the fat, then sucking the fat from his fingers. This time, when the boy offered him some, Mr. Paulsen declined.[86]

• Think carefully about where to do your writing. For a while, Judy Blume wrote in an office located above a bakery. However, at noon she was unable to resist buying and eating two glazed doughnuts, and at 3 p.m. she was unable to resist buying and eating two more glazed doughnuts. After a few months — and after gaining a few pounds — she started writing at home again.[87]

• When Sylvia Plath was a student in England, she did not make many female friends. One morning, she was cutting up her fried eggs, and another student asked her, "*Must* you cut up your eggs like that?" Ms. Plath replied, "Yes, I'm afraid I really must. What do you do with your eggs? SWALLOW THEM WHOLE?"[88]

• George Bernard Shaw was as thin as Lord Northcliffe was fat. Once Lord Northcliffe said to him, "The trouble with you, Shaw, is that you look as though there were a famine in the land." Mr. Shaw replied, "The trouble with you, Northcliffe, is that you look as if you were the cause of it."[89]

• When William Faulkner was awarded the Nobel Prize in Literature, Mississippi resident John Cullen wrote to the King of

Norway suggesting that the award presenters serve Mr. Faulkner some opossum meat and collard greens. The king sent back a very nice reply.[90]

• Famous philosopher George Santayana knew what he liked. Sometimes, he would pour wine over cake and then eat it. A friend once saw him do this. The friend was shocked, but he tried it, liked it, and continued to do it.[91]

• Mahatma Gandhi and the great Nobel-Prize-winning Indian poet Rabindranath Tagore once met, and Gandhi told him, "The suffering millions need only one poem — food."[92]

Free Speech

• Quite often people challenge books by Judy Blume; this means that people request that Judy's books be removed from libraries so that people cannot read them. Sometimes, these challenges result in her books being banned. At one school where her books were banned, students protested by wearing at school buttons that said, "Judy Blume for Principal" and "Judy Blume for President." By the way, when Judy's son and daughter were in elementary school, their mother's book *Are You There, God? It's Me, Margaret* was banned from the school library.[93]

• During high school, writer Nancy Garden discovered that she was a lesbian. She and her lover looked for books on homosexuality in the library, but those books were always checked out. Today, she realizes that those books had been censored — the books were always said to be checked out so that no one could read them. Ms. Garden is the author of *Annie on My Mind*, a young-people's novel about lesbians in love.[94]

• Distinguished Bible scholar Henry Cadbury, a Quaker, assisted in preparing the Revised Standard version of the New Testament. Unfortunately, many people disliked this book, and some of them even burned it. Mr. Cadbury merely said, "They used to burn the translators.

If now they only want to burn the translation, I guess we have made some progress."[95]

Friends

• Wisdom comes from many places. Pammy is the best friend of novelist Anne Lamott, author of *Imperfect Birds*. When Pammy was dying and in a wheelchair, Ms. Lamott asked her if she — Ms. Lamott — looked fat while wearing a certain dress. Pammy replied, "Annie, you really don't have that kind of time." Ms. Lamott says now, "I live by that." Ms. Lamott got something else from another friend, who lent her some "simple but fabulous gold hoops [earrings] from Guatemala." Ms. Lamott wore them, she liked them, and she told her friend, "You know, I won't be giving them back." Her friend said — sadly — that she realized that. Ms. Lamott wears the hoops often, and she says, "I still see her every few years, and I've always got the earrings, and we still laugh. You can see them in every author's photo of mine since my second book, *Rosie*."[96]

• Gonzo author Hunter S. Thompson had many friends on whom he could impose. One such friend was editor Shelby Sadler, who owns an excellent collection of reference books. He would often telephone her late at night or early in the morning and say something such as, "Shelby? Hunter. Tell me everything you know about the Rape of Nanking." In 1989, she really, really impressed the hard-to-impress gonzo writer by immediately knowing the main symptom — "elongated filiform papillae" — of a rare disease he was asking about: black hairy tongue disease. Within 10 minutes she was able to fax him photographs of three different sufferers of the disease.[97]

• Pablo Neruda and Rafael Alberti were both portly poets. They used to take walks together in Paris along the Seine and would use a complete set of the works of Victor Hugo in a bookstore to measure their girth. Mr. Alberti might say, "Good Heavens! I have already outgrown Volume V of *Les Misérables*!" And Mr. Neruda might reply,

"I haven't put on weight. My paunch juts out only as far as *Notre-Dame de Paris*."[98]

Gays and Lesbians

• When personal-finance guru Suze Orman realized that Kathy "KT" Travis was the right romantic partner for her, she did something extravagant. When Ms. Travis traveled back home, Ms. Orman sent her driver and car to meet her. The car was not empty: It was filled with gardenias — Ms. Travis' favorite flower. After Ms. Travis had returned home, the doorbell rang. A deliveryman was outside, holding a bunch of Casablanca lilies and wanting to know where to put the rest of the flowers — Ms. Orman had bought all the flowers in stock at a flower shop. (By the way, Ms. Orman does not want anyone to buy flowers for her. Why not? She says, "They [flowers] die.")[99]

• Alison Bechdel, a lesbian, draws the cartoon *Dykes to Look Out For* and is the author of important graphic novels. She frequently receives fan letters, including letters from very young children. Once, she received a letter from a nine-year-old who was impressed by her straight mother's lesbian friends and who wanted advice on how be a dyke. They corresponded for a while, and Ms. Bechdel explained that there is no single way to be a dyke. The nine-year-old's straight mother was very happy that Ms. Bechdel and her daughter were corresponding.[100]

• Before interviewing Edythe Eyde for a book about the life experiences of elderly lesbians, Zsa Zsa Gershick noticed she had a TV tuned to a daytime talk show about women with very large breasts. Seeing a woman with a size 44EEE chest, Ms. Gershick asked, "What in the world would anyone do with breasts that size?" Ms. Eyde winked and said, "Well, I don't know about you, but when I was younger, I would have had a hell of a good time!"[101]

• Gay African-American author James Baldwin did not believe in labels such as gay. When asked if he was gay, his usual reply was this: "I've loved a few men, and I've loved a few women." He once said, "It seems to me, in the first place, that if one's to live at all, one's certainly got to get rid of the labels."[102]

• When the very effeminate Quentin Crisp, author of *The Naked Civil Servant*, decided to emigrate from London to New York, he went to the American Embassy to get a visa. While there, he was asked, "Are you a practicing homosexual?" He replied that he didn't practice because he was already perfect.[103]

Chapter 3: From Gifts to Mishaps

Gifts

• For a while, Garry Wills and William F. Buckley were friends, and for a while, they were not friends. (By the time Mr. Buckley died, they were friends again.) When they were friends, Mr. Buckley gave Mr. Wills affectionately inscribed copies of his books. When they were not friends, Mr. Wills needed to reduce the size of his library so he could move it into smaller quarters, and he invited a used-bookstore owner to look at his books and buy what he wanted. The used-bookstore owner wanted, among other books, the books that Mr. Buckley had inscribed. Friends of Mr. Buckley used to find the books in the used bookstore, buy them, and send them to Mr. Wills along with a note berating him because he sold the gifts.[104]

• The family that Louisa May Alcott, author of *Little Women*, grew up in was poor but was also concerned about families who were poorer than they were. The Alcott family often ate two meals a day, giving away the third meal to an even poorer family. Louisa's father, Bronson, was thoroughly impractical. A kind neighbor once gave the Alcott family a load of wood, but Bronson gave it away to a family with an ill baby, even though his own family needed it. Fortunately, another neighbor arrived with another gift of wood for the Alcotts. Branson then told his family, "I told you we would not suffer."[105]

• The 18th-century French philosopher and writer Denis Diderot once received an elegant gift: a Chinese silk robe. He put it on and was delighted with it. But then he noticed that his slippers looked shabby, so he bought elegant new slippers. And when he wore the Chinese silk robe and sat down to write, he noticed that his desk looked shabby, so he bought an elegant new desk. And so it went until he had ended up completely renovating his entire writing room.[106]

• George Bernard Shaw once gave English entertainer Joyce Grenfell a present — seven postcard-sized photographs of himself that he had signed. When he gave her the present, he told her, "One for every day in the week and all out on Sunday. And don't sell them until I'm dead."[107]

Good Deeds

• When young-adult novelist Robert Cormier was in the 8th grade, his family's house burned down, and the suit that he was going to wear to his 8th-grade graduation ceremony burned up with it. Fortunately, the Cormiers' neighbors contributed money to buy clothing for them, and young Robert was able to wear a suit to his graduation ceremony. As an adult, Mr. Cormier did good deeds for other people. His novel *I Am the Cheese* contained a telephone number, which was his. He once received a call from a girl in a psychiatric institution who felt that she could identify only with the protagonist in the novel. Mr. Cormier says that he and she "had a long talk about how this Adam [the protagonist] in the book was really a reflection of her own life, even though the circumstances were much different." In the novel, Adam calls his friend Amy Hertz three times. That is the telephone number that the girl in the psychiatric institution called, and many other young people also called it. Sometimes they would ask for Amy. If Mr. Cormier answered the phone, he would pretend to be Amy's father. If his youngest daughter, Renee, answered the phone and was asked if Amy was there, she would say, "Speaking."[108]

• On New Year's Eve, Virginia Woolf and her husband, Leonard Woolf, also a famous author, attended a party for 12-year-old Angelica, their niece. All the attendees, including the Woolfs, were dressed as characters from Lewis Carroll's *Alice in Wonderland*. After the party was over, the Woolfs left, and in the street they saw a couple of men harassing an intoxicated woman. Police arrived, the two harassing men ran away, and the police began to question the intoxicated woman in an accusatory manner. Mr. Woolf stood up for the woman. Dressed in a paper hat and a green apron so he could portray the Carpenter of *Alice in Wonderland*, he told the police that they should leave the woman alone and instead find and question the men who had been harassing her. Mrs. Woolf, who was wearing the ears and paws of the March Hare, also joined in her husband's criticism of the police.[109]

• In 1933, seven-year-old Nelle Lee saw some older boys assaulting young Truman Streckfus Persons in what was supposed to be a game known as "Hot Grease in the Kitchen, Go Around!" In the game, the older boys stood in a line, crossed their arms, and dared someone to try to get past them and into a sandpit. Truman loved to be the center of attention, so he accepted the dare. Unfortunately, he was small, and the boys were able to keep him out of the sandpit and knock him to the ground and hit him. Nelle yelled, "Get offa him!" She also knocked the older boys off small Truman and then escorted him away from the older boys. The two became friends, and they became famous. Nelle Harper is better known as Harper Lee, author of *To Kill a Mockingbird*. Truman Streckfus Persons is better known as Truman Capote, author of *In Cold Blood*.[110]

• J.K. Rowling had some rough times in her life before hitting it big by writing the Harry Potter books. At one point, she and her daughter lived in a mouse-infested apartment. Unfortunately, she was in a poverty trap. She was unable to get a job unless her daughter was in childcare, and because she did not have a job she could not afford childcare for her daughter. Fortunately, she appealed to her lifelong friend Sean Harris, who helped her by giving her enough money for her and her daughter to move into a better, non-mouse-infested, one-bedroom apartment. Mr. Harris is an inspiration for the character Ron Weasley. Ms. Rowling says, "Ron Weasley isn't a living portrait of Sean, but he really is very Seanish."[111]

• When African-American author James Baldwin sent his first novel, *Go Tell It on the Mountain*, to the publisher Alfred A Knopf, Mr. Knopf was interested in it and wanted Mr. Baldwin to return to New York from Paris, France, in order to revise the novel. Mr. Baldwin was willing, but he lacked money to do that. Fortunately, a friend of his, Marlon Brando, who had become famous by starring in Tennessee Williams' play *A Streetcar Named Desire*, came through for him by lending him $500, and Mr. Baldwin came back to New York in April 1952. Mr. Baldwin said about Mr. Brando, "Race truly meant nothing to him. He was contemptuous of anyone who discriminated in any way."[112]

• Theodor Geisel, aka Dr. Seuss, gave money to good causes, including sending some high-school students in La Jolla, California, where he lived, to a Science Olympiad. The students had created a machine called the Scrambler that scrambled eggs by tossing them 10 meters into the air. Along with the money, he sent this note: "Scrambling has always been my favorite Olympic event."[113]

Halloween

• When Christopher Paul Curtis, author of *Bud, Not Buddy*, was a child, his mother worried about her children trick-or-treating, so instead of letting them go out for trick-or-treat, she made them dress up in Halloween costumes and go from room to room of their house. In each room, she would put candy in their bags.[114]

Husbands and Wives

• After writing her first novel, *The Outsiders*, S.E. Hinton became depressed and suffered from writer's block. It was her boyfriend who figured out that she was depressed because she wasn't writing. Therefore, he came up with an idea to make her start writing again. She would have to write two pages a day. He would stop by in the evening, and if she hadn't written two pages, they wouldn't go out. It worked. She wrote *That Was Then, This is Now*. Her publisher accepted it immediately. By the way, S.E. and her boyfriend, David Inhofe, got married. She wrote her third book, *Rumblefish*, on Thursday nights because that was when her husband played poker. S.E. lets her husband read her in-progress manuscripts because he always says, "That's nice, honey," which is the only thing she wants to hear when she is in the middle of writing a book. They had a son, whom they named Nick, and Nick contributed to two picture books she wrote for very young children: *Big David, Little David*, and *The Puppy Sister*. On Nick's first day of kindergarten, he met a boy named David. Coming home, he said to his father, "Dad, there's a kid in my class and his name is David like you and he has dark hair like you and he wears glasses like you. Is that you?" His father replied, "Sure, Nick, that's me. Every day I get little, and I go to school with you." S.E. helped her husband with the joke. Nick would come home and tell her what had happened at school — for example, that a child named Kelsey had thrown up. S.E. would telephone her husband and give him the information, and when he got home he would say to Nick, "Weren't you grossed out when Kelsey threw up?" This went on for almost a year. S.E. says, "We figured, heck, we'd given the kid something to tell the therapist when he's forty." *The Puppy Sister* is based on a puppy that S.E. gave Nick. A sibling rivalry broke out, and Nick once accused her of loving the puppy more than she loved him. And Nick once asked her when the puppy would stop being a puppy and turn into a person.[115]

• After writing *Bud, Not Buddy*, author Christopher Paul Curtis heard that it was being considered for both the Newbery Award, which is given to the best American children's book published each year, and for the Coretta Scott King Award. (Honor books are second-place winners.) He also heard that if he won either award, he would hear the news by telephone by 9 a.m. He woke up at 5 a.m. and was so excited that he cleaned the entire house. His wife, Kaysandra, took their daughter, Cydney, to school. At 9:15 a.m. his telephone rang, but since it was after 9 a.m. he thought that it was his editor calling to offer him sympathy. It wasn't his editor. Instead, it was a person telling him the very good news that his book had won the Coretta Scott King Award. At 9:32 a.m., his telephone rang again, and he heard the very good news that his book had won the Newbery Award. When his wife returned, he laid a trap for her, asking, "What if I won a Newbery Honor and a Coretta Scott King Honor, could I not do housework for an entire year?" She replied, "You'd have to win both the Newbery Award and the Coretta Scott King Award not to do housework for a year." He then sprang the trap — he had in fact won both the Newbery Award and the Coretta Scott King Award! However, he says, "She's not a woman of her word — I'm still doing housework!"[116]

• After Louis Sachar, winner of the Newbery Medal for his young-adult novel *Holes*, started publishing books for kids, he began to receive many letters from students at Davis Elementary School in Plano, Texas, who wanted him to visit their school. He remembers, "Some of the girls had written things like, 'Our cute, single teacher thinks you're really great!'" He did visit the school, and he did like the cute, single teacher, but he ended up marrying someone else at Davis Elementary: Carla Askew, the school counselor.[117]

• Tim Powers was visiting his friend the author Philip K. Dick one evening when Mr. Dick's wife, Tessa, and her brother started carrying out lamps and furniture. Mr. Powers asked Mr. Dick, "Phil, they're taking stuff. Is this OK?" Mr. Dick was used to being divorced, and he replied, "Powers, let me give you some advice, in case you should ever find yourself in this position. Never oversee or criticize what they take. It's not worth it. Just see what you've got left afterward, and go with that." Just then, his wife's brother said to them, "Could you guys lift your glasses? We want the table."[118]

• In 1981, horror writer Stephen King's wife, Tabitha, wrote her first book, *Small World*. She received $165,000 for the paperback rights, a huge sum for a first-time novelist, and she acknowledges that some of her success was made possible because she was the wife of a best-selling novelist. However, she also says, "I put 10 years into helping his career, so if his name helps me with mine, I think it's [fair]." By the way, Mr. King's beard is often seasonal — when it isn't baseball season, he shaves it off.[119]

• Madeleine L'Engle, author of *A Wrinkle in Time*, was married to her husband, actor Hugh Franklin, for forty years. The marriage ended only with his death. When both of them were in their sixties, he looked at her and exclaimed, "Darling! We're never had time for a mid-life crisis!" Ms. L'Engle says that he was correct: "Life was too busy. But we do have wonderful children and grandchildren."[120]

• Wendy Cope's second book of poetry, *Serious Concerns*, contains a number of what she calls "angry poems about men." At one reading, a woman told her, "Three of my friends left their husbands after they read your book." She replied, "Gosh, I hope they made the right decision." Her other volumes of poetry contain fewer "angry poems about men."[121]

• On his deathbed, German poet Heinrich Heine changed his will, leaving everything to his wife — provided that she remarried. Why? He explained, "When Matilda remarries, there will be at least one man who regrets my death."[122]

Illnesses and Injuries

• Critic Simon Barnes believes that the thrillers of Dick Francis are predictable, but that isn't a problem because in addition to being predictable they are predictably good. In fact, they make perfect reading on a transatlantic flight from London to New York. Mr. Barnes writes, "Three bloody Marys and a new Dick Francis and you're in New York before you know you've taken off." By the way, Mr. Francis was a jockey before he became an author. Like all jockeys, he was frequently injured, fracturing his collarbone six times, breaking his nose five times, and fracturing his skull once. Mr. Francis remembers one particular accident: "A horse put his foot right through my face, slicing my nose open. I had 32 stitches from above my eye to the end of my nose. The doctor was delighted because he could show the inside of a nose to all his students."[123]

• When Anthony Burgess was incorrectly diagnosed with brain cancer, he wrote five books in a year because he wanted his widow to be financially provided for after his death.[124]

Insults

• While in the company of Mark Twain, the French author Paul Bourget insulted all Americans by saying, "When an American has nothing else to do, he can always spend a few years trying to discover who his grandfather was." Mr. Twain replied, "And when all other interests fail for a Frenchman, he can always try to figure out who his father was."[125]

• Many people kiss and tell, but the novelist George Moore was once accused of something else. A woman named Susan Mitchell said about him, "Some people kiss and tell. George Moore told but did not kiss."[126]

Language

• The best comedians often have many skills — they not only make people laugh, but also master language, criticize what is bad, recognize what is good, give credit where credit is due, and think both well and deeply. For example, George Carlin read and admired the books of Robert S. McElvaine. About *Eve's Seed: Biology, the Sexes, and the Course of History*, Mr. Carlin wrote, "This impressive book ... will provide [an] invaluable source of inspiration ... regarding the huge issue of male/female roles and their impact on us. It's about time someone put men in their proper place: on the bottom." And Mr. Carlin provided this blurb for Mr. McElvaine's *Grand Theft Jesus: The Hijacking of Religion in America*: "If Robert McElvaine had been Jesus' lawyer, Pontius Pilate would have released him on his own recognizance."[127]

• Ian McEwan wanted to learn to speak correctly when he was young; therefore, he arranged for his best friend, Mark Wing-Davey, whom he calls "a rare and genuine middle-class type," to say the word "did" whenever Ian mistakenly said the word "done." One day, Ian gave an oral presentation in history class on the reforms of Pope Gregory VII. Ian mistakenly said the word "done," Mark said the word "did," and the history teacher became angry at what he thought was Mark's rudeness. Fortunately, Ian was able to explain what had happened.[128]

• Lesbian author Valerie Taylor was on Studs Terkel's radio program one day and she said the word "screw." One of the radio personnel said, "We'll have to blip out 'screw.'" Ms. Taylor responded, "I thought I was being nice. What I really meant was 'f**k.'" Afterwards, Studs sometimes asked Ms. Taylor as a private joke, "When are you gonna come on my show and say 'f**k'?"[129]

• Edward Gibbon wrote a massive history of the decline and fall of Rome. Once, Richard Brinsley Sheridan called Mr. Gibbon "luminous." When a friend later asked why he had chosen that particular word, Mr. Sheridan joked that he had made a mistake: "I meant voluminous."[130]

• Makeup — at one time aka paint — has been with us a long time. At a party, Voltaire asked Lord Chesterfield which of the women present — the French or the English — he thought were more beautiful. Lord Chesterfield punned, "I am no connoisseur in paintings."[131]

Letters

• When Stan Lee, creator of Spider-Man and the Fantastic Four, was a kid, he wrote his hero, Floyd Gibbons, who went on adventures and wrote a column for the *Chicago Tribune*. Mr. Gibbons wrote him back, something that truly impressed the young Stan Lee. Working at Marvel, he encouraged fan mail and he often wrote fans back, either in person or on the pages of the comic books he wrote. Mr. Lee says, "I wanted the fans to feel that they were part of the Marvel family. If I received a letter that started 'Dear Editor' and was signed [...] 'Charles Smith,' I would write back, 'Hiya Charlie!' I wanted it to sound friendly, and I signed all my replies 'Stan,' not 'the Editor.' I think it worked because when I met fans at conventions, they came up to me as though we were old friends. 'Hi, Stan, how are ya? I've always wanted to meet you.'" Actually, it was Mr. Lee's creations that got Marvel Comics fan mail. He says, "Before the Fantastic Four, we hardly ever got fan mail. Occasionally I might get a letter from somebody that said,

'I bought one of your comic books and one of the staples is missing. I'd like my ten cents back.' I would tack that letter up on the bulletin board and say, 'We've got a fan letter.' But after the Fantastic Four came out, we started to get genuine fan mail. At the start, a lot of the letters were written in pencil. After a few months, they were written in ink. A few months after that, we were getting typewritten letters and the return addresses were high schools and colleges."[132]

• In 1960, Madeleine L'Engle finished her novel *A Wrinkle in Time*. She knew that it was her best novel yet, but over 40 publishers rejected it, and she and her agent gave up sending it to publishers. Fortunately, Ms. L'Engle threw a tea party that was attended by John Farrar, part of the publishing company Farrar, Straus, & Giroux, and at a meeting after the party he took her manuscript. He read it, loved it, and agreed to publish it, even though his publishing company did not even have a juvenile line of books at the time. The novel became an immediate success, winning the prestigious Newbery Medal, which is given for the most distinguished children's book published during a year, and afterward Ms. L'Engle met many publishers who said to her, "I wish I'd gotten my hands on that book!" Frequently, Ms. L'Engle pointed out that the publishing company had looked at the book — and rejected it. One publisher refused to believe her until she showed him the rejection slip his company had sent her.[133]

• When asked who her guest at the Ritz would be if she could have anyone as a guest, crime novelist Patricia Cornwell, creator of the Scarpetta series, replied that she would have Allen Ginsberg as a guest, although the restaurant would actually be "Il Cantinori in New York or Davide in Boston." She explains that she is a fan of poets, and when she was a college student she wrote letters to several poets — "and darn if some of them didn't write me back. [Mr. Ginsberg's] letter in particular was outrageous, profane, and long, and I couldn't believe he would take the time to write a little nothing college student like me. I wish I could take him to dinner and thank him, and explain that his various uses of the f-word wouldn't shock me now the way they did back then."[134]

• Even as a young woman, American poet Emily Dickinson suffered from a lack of privacy in her own home. For example, her father made her read any letters she received out loud. After receiving a letter from her brother, she wrote him back about reading his letter out loud to the family. First, she had gone through the letter and self-censored it, marking through the places she didn't want to read out loud, then with her heart beating wildly, she read the letter to her family, pretending that she had not self-censored it, and her heart didn't stop beating wildly until she had finished reading the letter.[135]

• Jerry Spinelli, the author of *Crash* and *Wringer*, got many, many rejection letters when he was a young author, but he did not give up. Every time he finished a novel that no publisher would publish, he wrote another novel. Mr. Spinelli once noted that during his first 15 years of writing, he made only $200 from his writing. He also recommended that publishers send rejection bricks instead of rejection letters, noting, "Decades of work should not be able to fit into an envelope. You should be able to build a house with them."[136]

• Young-people's author Richard Peck has received many letters from the readers of his books. Some are funny, as when someone wrote, "Our teacher told us to write to our favorite author. Could you please get me the address of Danielle Steele?" Other letters are serious; for example, someone wrote to him about *Remembering the Good Times*, a novel that recounted a suicide and educated the readers about the warning signs of suicides. The person wrote, "The only trouble with your book is that I didn't find it in time."[137]

• Karyn McLaughlin Frist edited a book titled *"Love you, Daddy Boy": Daughters Honor the Fathers They Love*. Just as the title suggests, the book is a collection of reminiscences of loving fathers by loving daughters. The title comes from the way Ms. Frist's father signed his letters that each Monday he wrote to her when she was in college:

"Love you, Daddy boy." Her friends used to ask her, "So what did Daddy boy have to say today?"[138]

• M.E. Kerr, author of books for young adults, received many rejection letters when she was trying to be published. In fact, she once attended a sorority costume party dressed as a rejection slip. She wore a black slip on which she had attached many of the rejection letters she had received.[139]

Media

• In February 2009, the *Tucson Weekly* celebrated 25 years of existence. Since most alternative newspapers don't last that long, it was and is something to celebrate. Douglas Biggers and a friend named Mark Goehring started the newspaper. Mr. Biggers wrote in the newspaper's 25th-anniversary edition, "It should have died a quick and easy death, since it was started by two 24-year-olds with no money, limited experience and virtually no qualifications to assume the monikers of editor and publisher. The city had a nasty reputation for chewing up and spitting out all attempts to start publications that were alternatives to the daily papers. That the *Tucson Weekly* continues to thrive and can celebrate 25 years of publication is nothing short of a miracle." One of the miracles that kept the newspaper alive was that they never received a bill for printing it for the newspaper's entire first year of existence. They had asked for two weeks' credit, and they marveled as the two weeks' credit turned into 50 weeks' credit, during all of which time they were making the newspaper grow. At the end of the year, they contacted their printer and set up a meeting to discuss their credit situation. It was about time because they now owed over $100,000 in printing costs. They soon discovered why they had received a year's credit: An accounting clerk at the printer's offices did not want to confront them about their bill, so the clerk had let the credit continue. Mr. Biggers remembers, "The suits from Texas came to town soon thereafter, and the story ends with a lawsuit that was settled out of court after a series of misadventures with attorneys and a judge pro tem who I am convinced (and whose name I cannot recall) was a fan of the paper and somehow enabled us to prevail against formidable odds." In the end, the *Tucson Weekly* survived, which is something worth celebrating.[140]

• *Tucson Weekly* columnist Tom Danehy, whose columns are known for their use of the first person, original point of view, love of (most) sports, and sense of humor, has worked for a number of editors, including a woman editor who told him, "I don't like first-person stuff; I don't like your point of view; I hate sports; and I don't get your sense of humor. Frankly, I don't understand why you write for this paper. Your next column and all of the columns after that have to have solid reporting, no first-person and no humor. Otherwise, you're gone." His very next column was titled, "Tom Goes to the Golf Tournament and Goofs on People." He says, "I figured I'd go out big." He adds about the woman editor, "Fortunately, she ran afoul of others, too, and Doug [Biggers, the founder] got rid of her."[141]

• Early in the 20th century, the New York *Evening Graphic* was competing with the New York *Daily News*. Bernarr McFadden was desperately trying to increase the circulation of the *Evening Graphic*, but his newspaper's circulation lagged that of the *News* by a half million copies. Desperate, Mr. McFadden summoned his staff to a meeting, where they brainstormed ways to increase the circulation of the *Evening Graphic*. Mr. McFadden asked, "How is the *Evening Graphic* going to get more circulation?" An underling answered, "Publish it daily in the *News* as an advertisement."[142]

• Lots of people like to see their words in print. For example, in Liverpool, England, at one time was a paper called *Mersey Beat*. People were allowed to put personal ads in the paper, and so some members of the Beatles — Paul McCartney, John Lennon, and George Harrison — used to write little ads such as "Barry! Meet me behind the station" just in hopes to see them in print. Mr. McCartney remembers, "And then it would come out and we'd be like, 'Yeah! It got in!' Just seeing it there was a little kick."[143]

• Richard Foster, a popular Quaker author, was asked several times to appear on the *PTL Club* TV show, and in 1987 he did appear. However, instead of discussing his latest book, *Money, Sex, and Power*, he was asked instead to discuss an earlier book he had written that had the noncontroversial title *A Celebration of Discipline*.[144]

Mishaps

• Maya Angelou once visited Senegal, where a friend named Samia invited her to supper. While she was there, she noticed that none of the guests was walking on the carpet. This made her angry because, she says, "I had known a woman in Egypt who would not allow her servants to walk on her rugs, saying that only she, her family and friends were going to wear out her expensive carpets. Samia plummeted in my estimation." Therefore, to make a point, she walked back and forth a few times on the carpet as "[t]he guests who were bunched up on the sidelines smiled at me weakly." Later, she regretted her action. Servants rolled up the carpet she had walked on, put down a fresh carpet, and then put food and plates and eating utensils on it. Samia then said to her guests that in honor of Maya Angelou, she was serving a very popular dish from Senegal. The guests then sat on the carpet. Ms. Angelou realized that in her ignorance, she had been walking on her host's tablecloth, and she says that she was "on fire with shame."[145]

• R.L. Stine has written many, many scary books for kids in his *Goosebumps* and *Fear Street* series of horror novels. So what scares him? Actually, jumping into a swimming pool scares him. When he was a kid attending summer camp, he was placed in the beginners' swimming group, which was called the Tadpoles. To move up into the next higher group, the Turtles, a Tadpole had to jump into the swimming pool, then swim the length of the pool and back. When it was his turn to jump into the pool, he couldn't do it. Swimming back and forth in the pool was no problem, but jumping into the pool horrified him. He walked away as the other Tadpoles laughed at him. Today he says, "My [...] nephews think it's very funny. They're always teasing me and trying to get me to jump. They think it's funny that a horror writer is afraid to jump into a swimming pool."[146]

• Monty Python Terry Jones was friends with Douglas Adams, author of the *Hitchhiker's Guide to the Universe* books. One story that Mr. Adams used to tell was of being at a train station with a *Guardian* newspaper and a package of biscuits (British for cookies). He sat down with a cup of coffee and put down the newspaper. In the middle of the table was a packet of biscuits. Another man was already at the table, and he very calmly opened the packet of biscuits and ate one. Mr. Adams was annoyed but remained silent, and he ate a biscuit. The other man then ate a biscuit, followed by Mr. Adams eating another biscuit. Mr. Adams was still annoyed, but he made an effort not to glare at the other man. When it was time to leave, Mr. Adams stood up, picked up his newspaper — and discovered his packet of biscuits underneath the newspaper.[147]

• Leslie Goldman, the author of *Locker Room Diaries: The Naked Truth About Women, Body Image, and Re-Imagining the "Perfect" Body*, once had the interesting experience of receiving this email: "Jim O'Connor is writing a book about unattractive people who have faced the world and found happiness, a good job, and love. Can he interview you?" In fact, the email was so interesting that Ms. Goldman writes that when she read it she snorted "Jelly Bellies out of my nose." Another interesting experience came when she was a student. She came across a hippie who was stopping people and asking them, "Are you interested in becoming a writer or poet?" She swept on past him, and he yelled after her, "BEAUTY FADES! BUT YOUR WORDS WILL LIVE ON FOREVER!"[148]

• Ian Fleming, the creator of James Bond, attended Sandhurst military academy. The Duke of Cambridge, who was Queen Victoria's commander in chief, had visited Sandhurst when many of the officer-cadets were contracting venereal diseases and told them, "I understand that some of you young gentlemen have been putting yours where I wouldn't put my walking stick." Ian disregarded this advice, if he was ever aware of it, and quickly got gonorrhea. That, of course, is not the only mistake Ian ever made. After Ian published *On Her Majesty's Secret Service*, his friend, Patrick Leigh Fermor, reminded him that Pol Roger is never sold in half bottles — and it is the only champagne that is not sold that way.[149]

• Mishaps occur even to world-famous novelists. Brazilian writer Paulo Coelho once spent a year working as a correspondent in England, during which time he also wrote his autobiography, but when he returned to Rio de Janeiro, he accidentally left the manuscript of his autobiography in a London pub. Goodbye, one year's worth of autobiographical writing. Later, Mr. Coelho wrote an autobiography about his years practicing black magic and evil. However, his wife read the book and advised him to destroy it. He did destroy it, keeping only a chapter that did not deal with black magic and evil.[150]

• The earliest memory of novelist Zoë Heller, author of *Notes on a Scandal*, is when she was six years old and peed in a wastepaper basket at night because she didn't want to walk down the hall to the bathroom. And her most embarrassing moment is when she was six years old and her mother asked her, "Have you been peeing in the wastepaper basket?" By the way, Rosanna Greenstreet of *The Guardian* once asked her, "If you could bring something extinct back to life, what would you choose?" Ms. Heller replied, "Marlon Brando, aged 24."[151]

• Tony Hillerman wrote mysteries set in the west. Although vastly talented, he sometimes made mistakes in his novels. He once said, "I always put safeties on guns that don't have safeties and leave them off ones that do." One night at about 10 p.m. he received a call from a reader who told him, "I used to have a lot of respect for you until I've just been reading *Dance Hall of the Dead*. Don't you know deer don't have gall bladders?" Mr. Hillerman said that is the best telephone call from a reader that he has ever had.[152]

• As a schoolgirl, Joyce Grenfell, who later wrote and memorized her own monologues, appeared in a school production of the Shakespeare play *As You Like It*. She had only one speech to make, and since this was before she discovered Shakespeare, she had no idea what the speech meant and thus had a hard time trying to memorize it. Finally, she wrote the speech on her palm the night before the performance — because the ink was indelible, it stayed visible on her palm for several days.[153]

• When Virginia Woolf, née Stephen, was a small child, the famous novelist Henry James often visited her house. During intense discussions the famous novelist often leaned his chair back so that only two legs touched the floor. Virginia and his siblings hoped that one day he would lean back so far that he would tip the chair — and himself — over. One day, to the delight of the children, he did just that. Mr. James simply continued the discussion as he picked himself and the chair up.[154]

• People who use dog sleds a lot have to become used to accidents, since dogs take wrong turns, sleds tip over, and drivers fall off the sled and are left behind. Once, author Gary Paulsen was on a run with his sled dogs when he slipped and was dragged behind the sled. In a pocket, he carried wooden matches that lit and caught his pants on fire.[155]

• Children's book author Lois Lowry, a two-time winner of the Newbery Medal, appeared on *Jeopardy!* in the days when it was live. She remembers that the makeup artist darkened only one of her eyebrows, giving her a quizzical appearance.[156]

Chapter 4: From Money to Prejudice

Money

• William Blake made little money from his poetry and art, but he did not love money. He once said, "Were I to love money, I should lose all power of original thought. Desire of gain deadens the genius in man. My business is not to gather gold, but to make glorious shapes." However, occasionally he realized that he needed to make money. His wife, Catherine, who had a spirit kindred to his own, used to put whatever food was available on their dinner plates and serve it. Occasionally, Mrs. Blake would put an empty plate in front of her husband. Mr. Blake also believed that schools all too often instill conformity: "Thank God I was never sent to school / To be Flogd into following the Style of a Fool." Mr. Blake did have one other important opinion. He once showed a visitor the view through his window. Some children could be seen playing happily together, and Mr. Blake said, "That is Heaven."[157]

• In August 1966, Gabriel García Márquez finished writing *One Hundred Years of Solitude*. The manuscript consisted of 490 typed pages, and he and his wife went to a post office in Mexico City to mail it to a publisher in Buenos Aires. Unfortunately, mailing the entire manuscript cost 82 pesos, and his wife had only 50 pesos. (The family had little money because while Mr. Márquez was writing the novel, he did not have a paying job.) They mailed half of the manuscript, went home and pawned a few items, including a hairdryer, and then returned to the post office and mailed the other half of the manuscript. *One Hundred Years of Solitude* made Gabriel García Márquez internationally famous.[158]

• When Marvel Comics was acquired by a new owner, maven Stan Lee was worried about his job. Therefore, he was very happy when his new boss told him that he would be making triple what he had made before. However, being a worrier, he worried that perhaps he had misunderstood what his new boss had said, so he decided to wait until payday to see if he had understood his new boss correctly. Payday arrived, Stan Lee looked at his paycheck, the paycheck was triple what he made before, and Mr. Lee decided that he loved his new boss — and that he would still love his new boss even if someone told him that his new boss was an axe murderer![159]

• *New York Times* best-selling thriller author Sandra Brown has 70 million copies of her many novels in print. She regards her best purchase ever to be an IBM Display Writer, which she purchased after receiving a $12,000 loan from a bank. She remembers, "I'd published seven books that were written on a typewriter. I typed at least three drafts of each. I spent a lot of time typing, which is entirely different from writing. One day it occurred to me that I wasn't being paid to type, so I trotted off down to the bank and made my pitch. That banker, now in his 80s, still brags about that loan to anyone who'll listen. Bless you, Art."[160]

• John Bogle, the founder of Vanguard, tells a story about authors Kurt Vonnegut, Jr., and Joseph Heller. They attended a party together — a party hosted by a billionaire who could easily appear on one of the television programs dedicated to the lifestyles of the rich and famous. Mr. Vonnegut talked to Mr. Heller about their host, pointing out that their host had made more money that day than Mr. Heller had made from all of the many, many copies of the vastly successful book *Catch-22* that had ever been sold. Mr. Heller replied that that was OK with him because he had one thing that their host would never have: "Enough."[161]

• In high school, young-people's author William Sleator and Vicky, his sister, knew a student who studied and studied and got all A's. In fact, she studied so much that her parents worried about her and wanted her to get a B once in a while. Eventually, they offered her $25 for each B she got on her report card. However, they ended up keeping their money — their daughter kept right on studying and getting A's.[162]

• James Baldwin, author of *Go Tell It on the Mountain*, had a very good reason for wanting to become rich and famous. He grew up poor in Harlem, where his family was too frequently evicted from their apartment, and he spent a lot of time watching over the children in the family. He said, "I wanted to become rich and famous simply so no one could evict my family again."[163]

• When Barbara Kingsolver received a $300 check in 1982 from *The Virginia Quarterly Review*, which published her story "Rose-Johnny," she celebrated by buying many, many reams of paper — as many as she could carry. She also wrote in her diary — in the center of a page that was blank except for these words — "I am a writer."[164]

Mothers

• When she was a child, Joanna Kathleen Rowling, aka Jo, became friends with two kids in her neighborhood: a brother and sister named Ian and Vicki Potter. Ian liked hijinks and dares. He once dared Vicki and Jo to run through some wet cement — they did. Of course, Ian and Vicki's last name became the last name of J.K. Rowling's most famous literary creation: Harry Potter. As an adult, Ian read the Harry Potter books out loud to his children. He remembers how he, Jo, and Vicki would play dress-up when they were kids: "And nine out of ten times, it would be Joanne who had the idea, and she'd always say, 'Can't we be witches and wizards?'" J.K. Rowling's own last name has led to her having lots of nicknames: Jo Rolling Pins and Miss Rolling Stone. When she taught English as a second language in Portugal, her students sometimes sang the theme song from the TV series *Rawhide* to her: "Rolling, rolling, rolling … keep those wagons rolling!"[165]

• Due to her years of drug abuse, actress/writer Mary Woronov, one of the stars of Andy Warhol's *Chelsea Girls*, has knowledge that ought to be forbidden to anyone. For salacious details, read her memoir *Swimming Underground: My Years in the Warhol Factory*. One of the few funny things in her book of horror is a reference to eviction parties, in which a person being evicted from an apartment would invite destructive friends over for a party in which they would tear the apartment to pieces. She also recounts a brief acquaintance with a transvestite who wanted to send a photograph of himself in drag to his mother so she would know that he had turned out well and not trashy like some other drag queens. Ms. Woronov had a vision of an old lady opening the envelope, looking at the photograph, and then having a heart attack, but she advised the transvestite to go ahead and mail the photograph to his mother.[166]

• Maya Angelou's early life was difficult. When she was eight, her mother's boyfriend raped her, and she stopped talking. Fortunately, he was arrested and convicted. When she graduated from high school early, she gave her parents this note: "Dear Parents, I am sorry to bring this disgrace on the family, but I am pregnant." She gave birth to her son, Guy, when she was sixteen, and she worked to support him. The birth of her son was a gift from God, she said later. She knew that she would have to educate him, so she began to educate herself. Whenever he asked her a question she didn't know the answer to, she would research the answer to the question. Later, Ms. Angelou became the author of a critically acclaimed series of autobiographies that began with *I Know Why the Caged Bird Sings*.[167]

• When Barbara Kingsolver and her siblings were growing up, they sometimes performed a play that they named "The Boy Who Saved His Town by Putting His Finger in the Dike." The audience for the play was their mother, whom Barbara estimates sat through approximately "a hundred virtually identical productions," showing her enthusiasm each time. Barbara says, "We took rave reviews for granted." By the way, the Kingsolver children grew up on a farm, and farm children end up eating some of the animals they raise. Her mother made her a promise: They would not butcher any animal to which they had given a first name.

And her mother let her know which animals she could name and which she could not.[168]

• Arianna Huffington's mother supported her. When young Arianna expressed a desire to go to Cambridge University, lots of people told her that she would never go there, but her mother borrowed some money and flew Arianna and herself from Athens, Greece, to Cambridge, England, so that Arianna could visit the campus. Arianna went to school at Cambridge, and later she moved to London, where critic Bernard Levin mentored and taught her. He put this message on a plaque on her desk: "You can break every grammatical and syntactical rule consciously when, and only when, you have rendered yourself incapable of breaking them unconsciously."[169]

• Early in his career, Marvel comic-book maven Stan Lee wrote many, many comic-book stories, and he used a number of pseudonyms: Stan Martin, S.T. Anley, Stan Leen, and Neel Nats (Stan Leen spelled backwards). By the way, Mr. Lee's real name is Stanley Martin Lieber. Because he wanted to get out of comic books later so he could write the Great American Novel, he decided to break his first name in two for his comic-book writing byline and save his real name for the serious writing he would do later. Fortunately for comic-book fans, Mr. Lee's serious writing turned out to be his comic-book writing.[170]

• J.K. Rowling, creator and author of the Harry Potter books, was not as poor as perhaps the media has made her out to be when she was writing the first Harry Potter book, but she was a single mother who did lack money. One day, she visited another mother whose boy was roughly the same age as J.K.'s daughter. That little boy had a room full of toys, and J.K. remembers, "When I packed Jessica's toys away, they fitted into a shoe box, literally. I came home and cried my eyes out." Those feelings of depression are the kind that the Dementors give in the Harry Potter books.[171]

• Mary Effie Lee was serious about her writing. In fact, at age 11 she wrote a "novel" that was all of three chapters and four pages long. Actually, she is better known as Effie Lee Newsome, the name under she published collections of poetry for children such as *Gladiola Garden: Poems of Outdoors and Indoors for Second Grade Readers.* When she married the Reverend Henry Nesby Newsome, she took his last name and dropped her first name. Why? She explained, "Because four names in a row would be like the long row of houses on our street in Philadelphia."[172]

• When he was a child, Gary Paulsen spent time in the Philippines with his father, who was in the military, and with his mother. Once, they traveled down a river in a canoe to a lake. Young Gary fell overboard, but fortunately a young Filipino boy rescued him. Gary's mother held him tight for a while, relieved that he was still alive, and then she made him get back into the water, saying that if he didn't do it now, he would be afraid of the water. She played with him in the shallow water until he no longer felt afraid. The grown-up Gary enjoys sailing.[173]

• While growing up, comedian Carol Burnett never thought of herself as beautiful — and neither did other people. When young Carol told her mother that she wanted to be an actress when she grew up, her mother replied, "Why don't you write instead? You can always write, no matter how you look."[174]

Names

• Gore Vidal's name is a Russian phrase that, literally translated, means, "He has seen grief." However, author/critic Jonathan Raban asked his Russian housekeeper about it and discovered that it has a stronger meaning than you may suppose. She told him, "Yes, but it is worse than grief. It is terrible. A woman, she have five sons, her only children, they all are killed at once in the war — *gore vidal*! It has many, many meanings. 'I was beaten so much nothing hurts me any more' — *gore vidal*. Sometimes it is sarcastic: we say '*gore vidal*!' like Americans say 'F**k you!' It is very common. I use it all the time." (Mr. Vidal's name when he was a boy was apparently Eugene Luther

— but "Louis" appeared on his birth certificate. At age 17, he changed his name to "Gore" in honor of Senator T.P. Gore of Oklahoma, his maternal grandfather.)[175]

• Elliot S! Maggin wrote many stories featuring Superman and Green Arrow. How did he get the exclamation point in his name? The first time it was a typo, but an editor named Julius Schwartz saw and liked the typo, so it stayed. Another name story: Author Jayme Lynn Blaschke is a guy, but lots of people seeing his name in print assume that the name belongs to a woman. Mr. Blaschke once submitted a story to Gordon Van Gelder, editor of *The Magazine of Fantasy & Science Fiction*, but Mr. Van Gelder addressed his rejection letter to Ms. Blaschke. At a convention, Mr. Blaschke walked up to Mr. Van Gelder to introduce himself. Seeing Mr. Blaschke's name card, Mr. Van Gelder immediately began apologizing even before Mr. Blaschke began to speak. Mr. Blaschke says, "More offense was assumed, obviously, than actually took."[176]

• At Dartmouth, Theodore Giesel became editor of its campus humor magazine, *Jack O'Lantern*. Unfortunately, after he hosted a noisy party the night before Easter, he was ordered to quit the position. Nevertheless, he kept editing the magazine as always — and writing and drawing for it. To keep the college dean from knowing that he was still working as editor, he began to use a pseudonym — his middle name, Seuss. Later, he added "Dr." to his pseudonym and joked that he had saved his father a small fortune by not going to medical school, yet becoming a doctor.[177]

• Young-people's author Orson Scott Card, writer of *Ender's Game*, and his wife name their children after their favorite authors. Michael Geoffrey is named after Geoffrey Chaucer. Emily Janice is named after Emily Bronte and Emily Dickinson. Charles Benjamin is named after Charles Dickens. Zina Margaret is named after Margaret Mitchell. And Erin Louisa is named after Louisa May Alcott. By the way, when Orson was a child, he learned to read phonetically, and therefore he pronounced "knew" as "canoe." That is the day that he learned about silent letters.[178]

• Progressive journalist Molly Ivins' name was actually Mary. The nickname "Molly" came from her childhood habit of burrowing like a mole among the books in her bedroom. She was a true original, once naming a dog "Sh*t" — I suppose for reasons that would be obvious if I had been acquainted with the dog. She was a master of the comic putdown, once writing about politician Dick Armey, "If ignorance ever goes to $40 a barrel, I want drilling rights on that man's head."[179]

• Late in his life, George Plimpton started to suffer from the effects of a lifetime dedicated to poor diet and a fondness for alcohol — and the production of much fine writing. In 2003, he collapsed while drinking at the Brook Club. Paramedics arrived, recognized him, and one paramedic started slapping his face and saying, "Hey, George! Wake up!" The maitre d' of the Brook Club did not approve and said to the paramedic, "At the Brook Club, sir, we refer to him as Mr. Plimpton."[180]

• Ambrose Bierce was a very talented writer of short stories, a cynical man, and a native of Meigs County, Ohio. In his book *The Devil's Dictionary*, he gives many cynical, but funny, definitions of common words. One example: he defines *zoo* as a "place where animals from all over the world come to see men, women, and children behave like fools." Because of his great cynicism, Mr. Bierce acquired the nickname "Bitter Bierce."[181]

• When LeRoi Jones first became a successful African-American writer, his works seldom mentioned race. Therefore, when fellow African-American writer Langston Hughes wrote to him in 1959, he teased, "Hail LeRoi, I hear you are colored." Later, Mr. Jones changed his name to Amiri Baraka, and when people read his writing, which now focused on black themes, they had no doubt that he was "colored."[182]

• Adjusting to another culture can be difficult. Nobel Prize-winning poet Octavio Paz was born in Mexico, but when he was six years old, his family moved to the United States for a while. In school at lunchtime, young Octavio needed a spoon, but he didn't know the English word for spoon, so he used the Spanish word: *cuchara*. As a result, he acquired a nickname: His classmates called him "Cuchara."[183]

Nobel Prize

• Through a fight, Pablo Neruda learned that his poetry was becoming popular. Two young men were arguing on a dance floor, so Mr. Neruda told them to stop arguing and let the other people enjoy themselves. As the first young man turned and listened to Mr. Neruda, the second young man hit the first young man and knocked him unconscious. Later, as Mr. Neruda left the dance club, the second young man was waiting for him. Mr. Neruda thought that he would be beaten up, but the young man suddenly recognized him and asked, "Are you the poet Pablo Neruda?" Mr. Neruda admitted that he was, and the young man said that he and his girlfriend had memorized much of Mr. Neruda's poetry — the poetry was keeping them together. When Mr. Neruda's friends came out of the dance club soon afterward, they found the young man reciting Mr. Neruda's poetry. In 1971, Mr. Neruda received the Nobel Prize in Literature.[184]

• In 1934, people speculated that the great Jewish Ukrainian poet Chaim Bialik might win the Nobel Prize in Literature. Unfortunately, he failed to win. Fortunately, he was philosophical about the loss, saying, "I'm very glad that I didn't win the prize. Now everybody's my friend and feels sorry for me." He went on to speculate about what would have happened if he had won the Noble Prize: "Then I'm sure some of the very same people who are now so indignant on my account would have said, 'What's so wonderful about getting the Nobel Prize? Why, even that poet Bialik got one!"[185]

• When Gabriel García Marquez won the 1982 Nobel Prize in Literature, all of his native Columbia and the rest of Latin America rejoiced. Children from an elementary school in Mexico City, where he lived, walked to his house and sang a song to honor him. People honked at him when they saw him driving, and once, when his car stalled at a red light, someone joked, "Hey, Gabo, the only thing you're good for is getting the Nobel Prize."[186]

Old Age

• Jean Genet attended the 1968 Democratic Convention in Chicago, where the police chased him and many others. At one point, Genet turned around and showed a police officer that he was an old man, and the police officer went around him and chased other people. More police officers were coming, so Genet knocked on a door at random to seek shelter. A person inside the apartment asked, "Who's there?" Genet replied, "Monsieur Genet." As it turned out, the person inside the apartment was familiar with Genet and his literary work — in fact, he was writing his thesis on Genet.[187]

• Theodor Geisel, aka Dr. Seuss, seems to have been always filled with good humor. When he got old, he joked that being age 82 had not changed his life: "I surf as much as I always have! I climb Mount Everest as much as I always have!" Of course, he had never surfed and had never climbed Mount Everest. And his 45th book, *You're Only Old Once: A Book for Obsolete Children*, appeared on his 82nd birthday. He attended a book-signing event and signed books for a line of 1,300 fans, joking, "Thank God my name isn't Henry Wadsworth Longfellow!"[188]

Poetry

• Dorothy Day was a friend of poet W.H. Auden. Once, she participated in a protest and was arrested and put in the women's prison. Each Saturday, the women prisoners were allowed to take a shower. One Saturday, one of the prisoners — a prostitute — recited these lines by Mr. Auden that had recently appeared in *The New Yorker*:

"Hundreds have lived without love, / But none without water." Mr. Auden said, "When I heard this, I knew I hadn't written in vain!"[189]

• Nahum Sokolow (1859-1936) was the editor of the Hebrew daily *Ha-Zifrah*. Once a young man saw him and submitted a poem for publication. Sokolow read the poem, then asked, "Did you write this poem yourself?" The young man said he had written it. Sokolow then said, "In that case, I am delighted and surprised to see you because I was under the impression that Judah L. Gordon, the author of this poem, had been dead for 10 years."[190]

Politics

• In France (at least until recently), politicians and civil-service workers were expected to be well read. In 2006, French President Nicholas Sarkozy got book lovers angry at him when he suggested that civil service entrance exams should not include questions about such things as the 17th-century French novel *La Princesse de Clèves* by Madame de La Fayette. Lovers of the works of La Fayette immediately did such things as arrange public readings of *La Princesse de Clèves*. In addition, the writer Jacques Drillon suggested that since Mr. Sarkozy is not well read, citizens of France should perform the good deed of mailing him books.[191]

• The family of Argentine author Jorge Luis Borges was against the Perón dictatorship. His mother and his sister were arrested because they took part in a political protest against the Peróns. His mother was aged and so was allowed to serve her sentence at home — an armed guard stood by the door for a month. Norah, his sister, could have gotten out of jail by writing a letter of apology to Eva Perón, but she declined to do that. Instead, she stayed in jail and used the time to create portraits of the inmates, who were mostly prostitutes. She portrayed the inmates as angels.[192]

Practical Jokes

• At one time, novelist Nick Mamatas, author of *Under My Roof* and *Move Under Ground*, used to write term papers for students who were incapable of writing their own. These students would go to a business that sold term papers, and people such as Mr. Mamatas would write a term paper on any topic and at any length the student wanted. The topics were usually deadly dull, and so Mr. Mamatas found ways to make the writing less deadly dull. If he was writing a paper for a business class, he would use Marxists as his sources. If he had to write a paper on any topic in ethics, he would write about the ethics of buying term papers rather than being honest and writing them yourself. If he had to write a paper on any topic in literature, he would write about his own short stories and novels — he says that several students "rate me as their favorite author and they've never even read me, or anyone else." Whenever he had to write a paper that included personal experience, he would make up and write about the student's sexual oddities.[193]

• H. Allen Smith once received a letter from a man who wrote that he knew that the letter would not be read by Mr. Smith, but by a secretary. This insulted Mr. Smith, who had never had a secretary. The man continued to write in his letter that he wished that the secretary were young, pretty, and redheaded. Mr. Smith wrote back to the man, inventing a secretary in the process. In the letter, Mr. Smith wrote that the man must be psychic because she (meaning the fictitious secretary) was young, pretty, and redheaded — furthermore, she was willing to take a day *and a night* off from work to meet him and have a good time. Later, a telegram arrived for the "secretary," setting up a rendezvous at a hotel. Mr. Smith thought about telling the man the truth, but he decided that the man needed to learn a lesson, so he let him come to New York. Mr. Smith received no more annoying letters from the man.[194]

• J.R.R. Tolkien, author of *The Hobbit* and *The Lord of the Rings*, played many pranks during his life. As a first-year student at Oxford, he played the female character of Mrs. Malaprop in Richard Brinsley Sheridan's play *The Rivals*. He and the other actors visited a tea shop, wearing overcoats while on the train, but taking them off and revealing their costumes in the tea shop. Later, when he was an Oxford don, he would sometimes dress as an Anglo-Saxon warrior and, wielding an axe, chase after a startled neighbor. Also, during lectures he would say that leprechauns existed — to prove their existence, he would take out of his pocket and display a pair of four-inch-long green shoes. And when he was an old man, he would buy something and sometimes hand the storekeeper the money needed to buy the item — along with his false teeth.[195]

• Screenwriter and playwright Charles MacArthur was a good chess player, and he often played chess at his club. When he met someone new there, he would pretend to be chess grandmaster José Capablanca, affect a Spanish accent, then beat the newcomer at a game of chess. However, once he pretended to be Mr. Capablanca, but the newcomer handily defeated him, getting him in trouble without spending much thought about his moves and dashing off for a dip in the pool while Mr. MacArthur sweated and thought deeply about what move to make next. After the game was over, the newcomer introduced himself — he was the *real* José Capablanca.[196]

• A retired Navy officer once dined at the home of Theodore Giesel, aka Dr. Seuss, where he fell asleep after supper. The officer's coat was unbuttoned, revealing his stiff white shirt. This was not an opportunity to be missed, so Dr. Seuss decorated the white shirt with several drawings of fantastical creatures.[197]

Prejudice

• The college-educated father of Virginia Hamilton, famed author of books for young people, faced racial prejudice. He was African-American, and when he dressed himself in a suit and went to a bank where he had been told that a "suitable job" awaited him, he was handed a broom and a mop. He threw both the broom and the mop a long distance inside the bank before leaving. He then got a job managing food services at Antioch College. Virginia also faced racial prejudice. She graduated at the top of her high-school class, which should have resulted in a college scholarship for her, but the scholarship went to a white student instead. Therefore, she approached Jesse Triechler, the wife of a theater professor at Antioch. Both Jesse and her husband, Paul, knew that Virginia was highly intelligent, and they knew that she had written a play that she had produced in high school. Jesse got on the telephone and kept calling people until she found someone in New York who was willing to sponsor a scholarship for Virginia at Antioch. The scholarship paid for her tuition and for her room and board.[198]

• Playwright Tennessee Williams hated racism. In 1947, his *Glass Menagerie* played to all-white audiences in Washington, D.C. He tried to stop this from happening, but he was unable. Therefore, he wrote to *The New York Times* that "any future contract I make will contain a clause to keep the show out of Washington while this undemocratic practice continues." Mr. Williams could see the humor in life as well as the evil. In 1977 he was asked to leave the Shaw Theater in London because he kept laughing during a performance of *The Glass Menagerie*. Michael Billington writes that "his incessant hilarity at this memory of his own youth was disturbing the rest of the audience."[199]

Chapter 5: From Problem-Solving to Work

Problem-Solving

• In 1923, Argentine author Jorge Luis Borges self-published his first book: a 64-page volume of poetry titled *Fervor de Buenos Aires* (*Adoration of Buenos Aires*). Only 300 copies were printed, and Mr. Borges was not out to make money but instead to get noticed. He took 50 or 100 copies to Alfredo Bianchi, an editor of the literary magazine *Nosotros*, whose offices were frequented by the literati, many of whom left their coats in one of the offices. Mr. Bianchi saw Mr. Borges with the books and asked, "Do you expect me to sell these books for you?" Mr. Borges replied, "No. Although I have written them, I am not altogether a lunatic. I thought I might ask you to slip some of these books into the pockets of those coats hanging out there." Mr. Bianchi did just that, and some literary VIPs read Mr. Borges' book, and some of them wrote about the book. In that way, Mr. Borges started to get a reputation as a poet.[200]

• Fantasy author Terry Pratchett discovered the library at an early age, but he also discovered that children were given only four tickets, meaning that they could check out only four books at a time. Therefore, he asked the head librarian if he could help out on Saturdays. The head librarian was willing, and quickly young Terry had 146 library tickets because he wrote the tickets himself. Being an honorary librarian meant that he was an honorary adult, so he began checking out and reading all the books he could find on fantasy, and on all the subjects that looked like fantasy, such as folklore, and mythology, and ancient history, and so on. He says, "And so I got educated by one thing leading to another. What was nice was when facts I came upon began to cross-reference with others I had already learned, when a web of knowledge started to form."[201]

• When Andrea Levy was very close to finishing her novel *Small Island*, she worried about losing the document, although she carried three copies of it in her handbag and kept a copy in her car as well as kept one on her computer hard drive. Still, she worried, what if the house caught fire and burned down with her handbag in it and wind carried the flames to her car and burned it, too. The next morning she gave a friend a copy to keep for her. She says today, after publishing a number of novels, "If I go away I send a copy of my work to my agent asking him not to look at it, but should I not return, please to publish it posthumously. I am forever convinced that I am never going to get to the end of a book, or that I'm going to lose it. I am an extremely cautious person."[202]

• When Stan Lee came up with the idea for a superhero with the abilities of a spider — Spider-Man — he ran into a problem. His boss felt that people were afraid of spiders and so the superhero would not be popular. Mr. Lee decided to sneak a story about Spider-Man into the last issue of a comic book that had failed — after all, since the comic book had failed and would be discontinued, who would care what appeared in its last issue? Response to the new superhero — depicted on the cover — was both overwhelming and overwhelmingly positive, and Marvel had a new very popular superhero to bring it profits for decades to come.[203]

• While on an archeological dig in Lebanon with her husband, Max Mallowan, mystery writer Agatha Christie stayed for a while in a horrible house that was infested with mice that ran across her face as she tried to sleep. Fortunately, Mr. Mallowan's assistant, Hamoudi, was able to solve the problem by going to a man who owned a gifted cat. The man brought his cat to the mice-infested house, and at dinner, five times mice ran across the room, and five times the cat pounced, catching the mice. After five days, no more mice were in the house, and the cat was able to retire with the gratitude of Ms. Christie and her husband.[204]

• For a while, children's author Peg Kehret wrote advertising copy for a radio station. She had to learn to write quickly and with originality, and one trick she found to be very effective is the one she calls "Five Minutes of Nonstop Writing." She found that if she wrote for five minutes nonstop, she would come up with an idea she could use — even if she started the five minutes by typing, "I don't know what to say" over and over.[205]

• When horror writer Stephen King was in high school, he satirized the official school newspaper with his own publication, the *Village Vomit*. Because he made fun of some teachers by name, the school officials were not happy, but they found an original way of solving what they felt was a problem — they got Stephen a job with the town newspaper writing sports articles so he had a respectable outlet for his writing talent.[206]

• While writing his horror novels, Stephen King likes to listen to rock music. Unfortunately, the rock-playing radio station in his hometown of Bangor, Maine, faced financial problems and was on the verge of switching to a different format of music. To make sure that the radio station kept playing rock music, Mr. King bought it.[207]

• The parents of Tamora Pierce were readers, and they encouraged her to read. However, they did not want her to read one book: a book about some English schoolgirls who start a brothel! Tamora sat in the living room with some Sunday funny pages in front of her — which she was using to hide the forbidden book she was reading instead of the funnies.[208]

• When Harper Lee, future author of *To Kill a Mockingbird*, first went to New York City to be a writer, she found an interesting way to get money for coffee and pie. She used to hit the heads of parking meters until they disgorged quarters, which bought a lot more then than now.[209]

• When novelist Walter Tevis (author of *The Hustler*, *The Color of Money*, and *The Man Who Fell to Earth*) was in the United States

Navy, the sailors would wash their jeans by tying them to a rope, then dragging them behind the moving ship.[210]

Public Speaking

• Young-people's author Walter Dean Myers once spoke at a school to some very young girls, one of whom said to him, "You're not that much!" At first, he was shocked, but then he realized exactly what she meant. In fact, he had felt the same when he was young and had seen the poet Langston Hughes being interviewed in Harlem. She meant that he was "a real person," Mr. Myers says. "If I can give kids an idea that I'm an ordinary person who is doing something that they like a lot, that's a wonderful thing." In fact, Mr. Myers is a real person. When he was young, his stepfather gave him a present: a manual typewriter. For a while, Mr. Myers typed nothing except "I hate this typewriter" on it, but then he started using it to write stories and poems.[211]

• Art Petacque and Hugh Hough won the Pulitzer Prize in 1974 for their coverage of the Valerie Percy murder case. They were a good team. Mr. Petacque had great sources, although no one ever saw him write anything. Mr. Hough lacked sources, but he knew how to write well. Mr. Petacque would come into the newspaper and talk to Mr. Hough, who would type while saying things such as "You're kidding!" When they won the Pulitzer Prize, Mr. Hough was playing golf. Without his partner, Mr. Petacque walked into the newspaper, received a standing ovation, and then stood on a desk, bowed to everybody, and said, "I only wish Hugh Hough was here to tell you how happy I feel."[212]

• While on a lecture tour, Mark Twain got a shave in a local barber shop. The barber knew that he was shaving a stranger, but he didn't recognize Mr. Twain, so he said, "You've come into town at the right time. Mark Twain is lecturing tonight." When Mr. Twain said that he was planning to attend the lecture, the barber asked if he had bought his ticket yet. Hearing that he had not, the barber said that he would have to stand, as most of the tickets were already sold. Mr. Twain sighed, then said, "That's my luck. Whenever that fellow gives a lecture, I always have to stand."[213]

• Food writer Peg Bracken was lecturing about cooking with onions (and the associated tears) before a Michigan audience when a woman seated in the back called to her, "You shut your mouth." This was unsettling — until she realized that the woman was merely trying to tell her that if she wanted to chop onions without her eyes tearing up, the solution was to chop the onions while keeping her mouth tightly closed.[214]

• Harold Ross, editor of *The New Yorker*, disliked speaking in public. Once he was given a surprise award and had to make an impromptu speech. He rose to his feet, faced the audience, feebly uttered, "Je-sus," then sat down. Frank Sullivan, who was seated next to him, said, "Your speech was too long, Ross. I got bored after the first syllable."[215]

• In 1985, American novelist Don DeLillo won the National Book Award for his novel *White Noise*. His acceptance speech was brief: He simply stood up and said, "I'm sorry I couldn't be here tonight, but I thank you all for coming."[216]

Religion

• Reverend Merrifield was the grandfather of Philip Pullman, who wrote the *His Dark Materials* trilogy. He told young Philip about a friend of his, named Fred Austin, with whom he had served in World War I. Mr. Austin went to war leaving an infant daughter behind. When he returned home, his daughter was a few years older, and she did not recognize this stranger who had entered her life, and so she ran from him. Eventually, of course, she learned that this man, her father, loved her and so she no longer ran from him. Mr. Pullman wrote much later, "When Grandpa told that story, he said that God would appear to us like that; at first we'd be alarmed and frightened by him, but eventually we'd come to trust his love." Mr. Pullman loves the classics, and he found a similar story to that of Mr. Austin in an ancient Greek epic poem: Homer's *Iliad*. In Book 6, Hector returns home to Troy, where he sees his wife and son. His son is frightened by Hector's helmet, but when Hector removes his helmet, his son is no longer frightened. Mr. Pullman grew up to become an atheist, and he says, "Between my childhood and now, I've lost sight of God, but Hector the Trojan prince and Fred Austin the Devonshire soldier are still brightly alive to me, and so is Grandpa."[217]

• When novelist Anne Rice was a youngster, her mother had a good way to get her out of bed for Mass: "The body and blood of Christ is on that altar — now get out of that bed!"[218]

Research

• While Paul Zindel, the author of such young adult novels as *The Pigman*, was researching a book in England, he asked people everywhere he went, "Did anything unusual ever happen here?" People at the Haunch of Venison, a 16th-century inn, replied, "Yes. We were doing renovations four years ago, and we found a severed hand in the wall." The inn's proprietors display the severed hand, now mummified, under glass at the bar.[219]

• Russell Freedman, author of many nonfiction books for teenagers, lives in an apartment in New York City. While doing research for his book *Martha Graham: A Dancer's Life*, he discovered that some of the people who had danced for her lived in his apartment building — to interview them, he simply rode the elevator to their floor.[220]

• Children's book author Peg Kehret does a lot of research for her books, including mysteries. She once went to a library and borrowed so many books about poison that the librarian grew nervous and asked to see her ID.[221]

Revenge

• *Tucson Weekly* columnist Tom Danehy dislikes it when one vehicle takes up two parking spaces. He also does something about it. One thing he has done is to buy a bag of ice and lodge it under the offending vehicle's right rear tire. Why? Tom explains, "When he [the driver] went to back out, it had to have made the most God-awful noise, causing the slamming of the brakes and the p*ssing of the pants." One day, he was going to throw his trash in the bed of an offending truck, but he had cleaned his vehicle the day before. So he got a tube of Icy Hot out of his glove compartment and smeared some of it on the handle of the driver's door of the offending vehicle. Tom says, "I'm really hoping that Billy Jim Bob had to adjust his *chonies* [testicles] after climbing into that beast."[222]

• Even before Jack Kerouac, author of *On the Road*, got published, he was a good writer. One of his early girlfriends, Edie Parker, got angry at him one day, so she made copies of the first love letter that he had sent to her and sold them for $1 each to servicemen who apparently wanted to copy the letter, sign their own names to it, and send it to their own girlfriends. Ms. Parker made $50.[223]

Sex

• Celebrated homosexual wit Quentin Crisp used to live in a house with several tenants, including a woman who would frequently bring home men and keep everyone up with her screams of sexual ecstasy. Eventually, she turned religious and lectured the other tenants on their lack of morality. Mr. Crisp told her one day, "I think I preferred you when you were a nymphomaniac."[224]

• James H. Billington, the 13th Librarian of Congress, spent his life reading and writing and raising a family rather than engaging in gardening. When his wife told their young daughter the facts of life — that a baby comes from a seed that Daddy planted in Mommy — the young daughter exclaimed, "That's IMPOSSIBLE! Daddy has never planted a single seed in his entire life!"[225]

Travel

• When Stephenie Meyer was searching for a location in which to set *Twilight*, a novel about a teenaged girl named Bella Swan who falls in love with a vampire named Edward Cullen who has been 17 years old for over a century, she researched the rainiest spot in the United States and discovered the Olympic Peninsula, and a little town called Forks, in the state of Washington. This became the setting for her novel, the first in a very popular series of novels, and a place that many tourists are starting to go to. The residents of Forks mainly enjoy the attention. When Forks Chamber of Commerce Director Marcia Bingham asked a couple of educators, David and Kim McIrvin, to allow their home to be designated as the Swans' home, they agreed. (Bella's home has two stories, and the McIrvins' home is the only house with two stories on their block.) A sign that says, "Home of the Swans," is out front. Carlisle Cullen is the fictional vampire who brought the family of vampires together. He is a doctor, and if you go to the Forks hospital, a parking spot has a sign that says, "Dr. Cullen: Reserved Parking Only."[226]

• Noah Webster is famous for his spelling book and for his dictionary. Because during and for a while after the American Revolutionary War, the British were the bad guys, he changed some English spellings to create American spellings. For example, *colour* became *color*, and *musick* became *music*. He also invented the word *demoralize*. He had great accomplishments, and he had great pride. When he visited Philadelphia, Benjamin Rush, a famous physician, said to him, "I congratulate you on your arrival in Philadelphia." Mr. Webster replied, "You may, if you please, sir, congratulate Philadelphia upon the occasion!"[227]

• A friend of food writer Peg Bracken's once made the climb up Fujisan, but she was bitterly disappointed. The travel books had promised her a breathtaking experience, but she saw trash lining the path up the mountain, and she was bothered by the steady line of 30,000 people all climbing up the mountain. Her husband, who had not read the travel books, felt the experience was breathtaking — he was amazed by the view.[228]

Typewriters

• Frederick Forsyth has written many novels, including *The Day of the Jackal*. How does he write? The same way he has written for 50 years, he says: "With a typewriter." One of those typewriters — a portable with a steel case — has seen a lot of action, and it demonstrated a great superiority over computers: "It had a crease across the lid which was done by a bullet in Biafra. [Mr. Forsyth was a foreign correspondent in the 1960s.] It just kept tapping away. It didn't need power, it didn't need batteries, it didn't need recharging. One ribbon went back and forward and back until it was a rag, almost, and out came the dispatches." Of course, typewriters have other advantages over computers. Mr. Forsyth points out, "I have never had an accident where I have pressed a button and accidentally sent seven chapters into cyberspace, never to be seen again. And have you ever tried to hack into my typewriter? It is very secure." And, of course, typewriters have yet another advantage over computers: tangible words. Mr. Forsyth says, "I like to see black words on white paper rolling up in front of my gaze."[229]

• Lois Lowry's first novel was *A Summer to Die*, which she sent to Melanie Kroupa, an editor at Houghton Mifflin Publishers. Instead of leaving for a scheduled vacation, Ms. Kroupa stayed in her office and read the entire book in one sitting, then shouted in a hallway, "We have to publish this!" Good choice. Ms. Lowry has won two Newbery Medals: one for *Number the Stars*, and one for *The Giver*. By the way, one good thing that came about from the publication of the novel was an important gift. She had typed the novel on a manual Smith Corona typewriter that her father had given her when she was 13 years old. To celebrate the publication of her first novel, he gave her an electric typewriter.[230]

Valentine's Day

• American poet Emily Dickinson was a nonconformist throughout her life. In 1849, when she was 19 years old, she attended the Mount Holyoke Seminary in South Hadley, Massachusetts. The head of the school, Miss Mary Lyon, told the students that Valentine's Day cards were foolish and that the students weren't allowed to send them. That February, Ms. Dickinson mailed more than 150 Valentine's Day cards.[231]

War

• Yoshiko Uchida and her family heard the news on the radio that Japan had attacked Pearl Harbor on Dec. 7, 1941, but they didn't believe it. Because Yoshiko was worried about taking her final exams at the University of California at Berkeley, she left her home to study at the library. When she returned home, she discovered that her father had been taken away for questioning and that FBI men were in her family's living room. The Uchidas and 120,000 other innocent Asian Americans were forced to leave their homes and be herded into internment camps on American soil — without a trial. At Tanforan Racetrack, the Uchidas lived for five months on four cots in a small and dark horse stall that stank of manure, then were assigned to the internment camp at Topaz, Utah. Yoshiko did graduate from Berkeley — with honors. Her diploma was delivered by mail to "stall number 40." Later, she became the renowned author of *Journey to Topaz*.[232]

• David Thomson, the historian and critic and author of the *New Biographical Dictionary of Film*, was a child during World War II. He lived in London, but his mother tried to take him to live in the country because Adolf Hitler was dropping bombs on London. It didn't work out, though, because David objected to the rural privy he had to use. When he asked his mother to take him back to London, he told her the reason why he wanted to go back to London. She replied, "You know what? Even if one of Mr. Hitler's specials came through the window, I'd rather be sitting on a nice lavatory than in that privy. This war is being fought for civilization, and if a proper bathroom doesn't count as part of that, then I don't know what does." And back to London they went. (Mr. Thomson writes that London was "where people gambled with bombs for a few moments of scented comfort.") [233]

• World War I helped Cambridge University in an unusual way. The university owned some stock in a steel company that rose in value with the war. Selling the stock at a high price, Cambridge University used its war profits to renovate an apartment used by poet A.E. Housman.[234]

Work

• Anna Sam worked for eight years as a check-out girl in a supermarket in France, then wrote the book *Les tribulations d'une caissière* (*The Trials and Tribulations of a Check-Out Girl*) about her experiences there. For example, occasionally a French mother would point to Ms. Sam and tell her child, "You see, darling, if you don't work hard at school, you'll become a *caissière* [check-out girl] like the lady." Whenever that happened, Ms. Sam informed the mother that she had had five years of education at a university. Unable to find a good job after graduation, she had taken the job at the supermarket. She says, "There are a lot of students with literary, sociology or artistic degrees in supermarkets in France. Not many of them really want to become check-out workers." Of course, France being France, even supermarkets are erotic locales. Ms. Sam says, "You would be surprised at the number of kisses in the aisles … at hands on bottoms in front of the frozen goods, at breasts caressed in the woman's lingerie [section]."[235]

• When poet Lawrence Ferlinghetti moved to San Francisco, he submitted some translations of poems by Jacques Prévert, and Pete Martin accepted them for publication in *City Lights* magazine. Mr. Martin had the idea of starting a bookstore to sell paperback books, which were at the time sold mostly in drugstores. One day, Mr. Ferlinghetti was driving back home from his painting studio, and he saw a man putting up a sign that said "City Lights Pocket Book Shop." He stopped, introduced himself to the man, who was Mr. Martin, and learned that Mr. Martin needed more money to get the bookstore started. Mr. Martin had $500, and Mr. Ferlinghetti had $500, and together they started the bookstore. Of course, City Lights published many of the Beat poets and writers, including Allen Ginsberg (*Howl and Other Poems*) and Jack Kerouac. Mr. Ferlinghetti says, "I could have driven around to get to my house by another block, and I never would have stopped there. My whole life would have been different."[236]

• Daniel Handler, author of the *A Series of Unfortunate Events* books, has a son whose birth helped him write the book series because suddenly he started thinking about all the unfortunate events that could happen to a child. He explains, "In the first year of a child's life, all the parents do is brainstorm terrible things that can happen and ways to avoid them, so suddenly I had a much longer list of horrible things than before — that came in handy." As a five-year-old, his son came up with a good description of what Mr. Handler's job became after he stopped writing the *A Series of Unfortunate Events* books — the series ended with volume 13 in 2006. He saw his father narrate *The Composer is Dead* (a child's introduction to the musical instruments of a classical orchestra; words by Daniel Handler, and music by Nathaniel Stookey), and then said that his father's job was getting angry on stage. Mr. Handler says, "It's not a bad description — actually it's very concise. I just might start telling everyone that's what I do."[237]

• When young-people's author Richard Peck was drafted to serve as a soldier during the Korean War (although he actually served in what was then West Germany), he soon discovered the value of literacy. He had a college degree, and he knew how to write and how to type, so he got a relatively cushy job. He says, "If you can type, spell, and improvise mid-sentence, you can work in a clean dry office near a warm stove." This is, of course, better than being "in a moist foxhole staring through barbed wire at an East German soldier who's staring back at you." He got another cushy job by writing sermons. He slipped the first sermon unnoticed under the chaplain's door. That Sabbath, the chaplain delivered the sermon. The next time Mr. Peck slipped a sermon under the chaplain's door, he made sure he was caught. The chaplain immediately made him his assistant.[238]

• Authors have many ways to come up with ideas to write about. John Cheever once complained that the tables in a certain restaurant were too far apart. Why was that a problem? He explained, "Now I can't eavesdrop on any of the conversations." By the way, being a writer may have saved his life. He enlisted in the United States Army in 1942, the same year that he published *The Way Some People Live*, his first collection of short stories. A major who was also an MGM executive had Mr. Cheever transferred to another unit where he worked as a writer. The unit that Mr. Cheever transferred out of suffered many, many casualties while fighting in Europe at the end of the war.[239]

• For children's author Jane Yolen, writing and books can be magical. She was writing one book when a group of elves appeared in her mind. She told them, "No elves in this book. Go away." They replied, "We're here." She says, "I was blocked for three weeks until I figured out why they were there." A nurse once sent her a letter to say that she had read one of Ms. Yolen's stories to a young, dying girl. She wrote that "the story had eased the little girl through her final pain." Ms. Yolen says, "The story did that — not me. But if I can continue to write with as much honesty and love as I can muster, I will truly have touched magic — and passed it on."[240]

• Like many authors, Dennis Lehane, who wrote *Mystic River* and *Gone Baby Gone*, both of which became movies, has had many jobs. He has been a counselor for abused children, driven limos, loaded tractor-trailers, parked cars, and — of course — waited tables. He says about his jobs, "Everything was based on the idea of taking the best possible job for me to be a writer with." For example, "Limos were phenomenal. You drive people somewhere and you wait for them for four hours." And, of course, while you wait, you write.[241]

• Mario Puzo wrote for men's adventure magazines before becoming a famous novelist. Once, because he was short of money, he asked Marvel Comics maven Stan Lee if he could write a comic-book story for him. Unfortunately, he came back to Mr. Lee without a story because writing it was too hard. He said, "I could write a novel in the time it would take me to figure this damn thing out." As if to prove his point, he sat down and wrote *The Godfather*.[242]

• The home office of children's author Walter Dean Myers has wallpaper that a child would enjoy — it is decorated with airplanes. In fact, the room used to be the nursery for his son Christopher, but when Christopher became too old for it, Mr. Myers moved out the nursery furniture, moved in the office furniture, hung up a picture of blues singer Billie Holiday, and went to work. The airplane-decorated wallpaper does not bother Mr. Myers.[243]

• Robert Bloch, the author of such books of horror as *Psycho*, on which the Alfred Hitchcock film is based, actually had a wonderful sense of humor. Early in his career, he published a story in *Weird Tales*, which paid a penny a word. In his autobiography, *Once Around the Bloch: An Unauthorized Autobiography*, he writes that he thought "if I could step up my output, perhaps in five or six years I'd make enough money to starve to death."[244]

• Sylvia Plath worked hard to be a writer. She once spoke about wearing out the roller of her typewriter in only one year. This astonished David Ross, who was a friend of Ms. Plath's husband, Ted Hughes. Mr. Ross had the same make of typewriter that Ms. Plath had — an Olivetti 22 — and its roller had shown no signs of wearing out — or even of wear — after many years of use.[245]

• Even after publishing her first children's book, *Busybody Nora*, Johanna Hurwitz wondered if she had really arrived. However, when she brought her second book, *Nora and Mrs. Mind-Your-Own-Business*, to her publishing house, her editor told her, "You're one of us now." Ms. Hurwitz says, "That's when I really knew that being a writer was not a fantasy anymore."[246]

• Humorous poet Oliver Herford used to work for *Life*. Apparently, he was conscientious about his work, as when he needed his shoes polished he often told the bootblack to shine just one shoe as he hadn't much time. In addition, Ms. Herford sometimes thought about working at home, but decided against it as he would have had to clean out his desk.[247]

• Neil Gaiman, author of *Coraline*, can write almost anywhere. When his father died, he took a plane to England, and he started writing during the trip. As the plane was beginning to land, his daughter told him, "Dad, you have to put that away now." He replied, "I don't want to stop writing — I have to find out what happens!"[248]

• At one time, Amy Tan, author of *The Joy Luck Club*, was a business writer, making lots of money while working 90 hours per week. She wasn't happy, so she started seeing a therapist — she soon stopped because during the sessions the therapist kept falling asleep![249]

• Journalist Heywood Broun once covered a labor dispute in which mine workers wanted a 40-hour week, which the mine owners opposed. A mine owner asked, "What will the miners do with all their free time?" Mr. Broun spoke up: "I'd suggest polo."[250]

Appendix A: Bibliography

Albert, Lisa Rondinelli. *Lois Lowry: The Giver of Stories and Memories*. Berkeley Heights, NJ: Enslow Publishers, Inc., 2008.

Allen, Everett S. *Famous American Humorous Poets*. New York: Dodd, Mead & Company, 1968.

Allen, William Rodney, editor. *Conversations with Kurt Vonnegut*. Jackson, MI: University Press of Mississippi, 1988.

Bailey, Paul, editor. *The Stately Homo: A Celebration of the Life of Quentin Crisp*. London: Bantam Press, 2000.

Baughan, Michael Gray. *Charles Bukowski*. Philadelphia, PA: Chelsea House Publishers, 2004.

Bedard, Michael. *William Blake: The Gates of Paradise*. Toronto, Ontario: Tundra Books, 2006.

Benchley, Nathaniel. *Robert Benchley*. New York: McGraw-Hill Book Company, Inc., 1955.

Blaschke, Jayme Lynn. *Voices of Vision: Creators of Science Fiction and Fantasy Speak*. Lincoln, NE, and London: University of Nebraska Press, 2005.

Bockris, Victor. *With William Burroughs: A Report from the Bunker*. New York: Seaver Books, 1981.

Bracken, Peg. *But I Wouldn't Have Missed It for the World!* New York: Harcourt Brace Jovanovich, Inc., 1973.

Brackett, Virginia. *Restless Genius: The Story of Virginia Woolf*. Greensboro, NC: Morgan Reynolds Publishing, Inc., 2004.

Bredeson, Carmen. *American Writers of the 20th Century*. Springfield, NJ: Enslow Publications, Inc., 1996.

Burshtein, Karen. *Walter Dean Myers*. New York: The Rosen Publishing Group, 2004.

Campbell, Kimberly. *Richard Peck: A Spellbinding Storyteller*. Berkeley Heights, NJ: Enslow Publishers, Inc., 2008.

Carter, David. *George Santayana*. New York: Chelsea House Publishers, 1992.

Church, Carol Bauer. *Carol Burnett: Star of Comedy*. Minneapolis, MN: Greenhaven Press, Inc., 1976.

Clarke, Nzingha. *Karen Hesse*. New York: The Rosen Publishing Group, 2006.

Clemens, Cyril. "An Evening with A.E. Housman." Webster Groves, MO: International Mark Twain Society, 1937.

Clower, Jerry. *Stories From Home*. Jackson, MI: University Press of Mississippi, 1992.

Coelho, Paulo. *Confessions of a Pilgrim*. Interviews by Juan Arias. Translated by Anne McLean. London: HarperCollinsPublishers, 2001.

Compson, William. *J.K. Rowling*. New York: The Rosen Publishing Group, 2003.

Crampton, Nancy, photographer. *Writers*. New York: The Quantuck Lane Press, 2005.

Daniel, Susanna. *Jane Yolen*. New York: The Rosen Publishing Group, 2004.

Daniel, Susanna. *Karen Cushman*. New York: The Rosen Publishing Group, 2006.

Dean, Tanya. *Theodor Geisel (Dr. Seuss)*. New York: Chelsea House Publishers, 2002.

Dolin, Sean. *Gabriel García Marquez*. New York: Chelsea House Publishers, 1994.

Dommermuth-Costa, Carol. *Agatha Christie: Writer of Mystery*. Minneapolis, MN: Lerner Publications Company, 1997.

Dommermuth-Costa, Carol. *Emily Dickinson: Singular Poet*. Minneapolis, MN: Lerner Publications Company, 1998.

Donaldson, William. *Great Disasters of the Stage*. London: Arrow Books, Limited, 1984.

Epstein, Lawrence J. *A Treasury of Jewish Anecdotes*. Northvale, NJ: Jason Aronson, Inc., 1989.

Fager, Chuck. *Quakers are Funny! A New Collection of Quaker Humor*. Falls Church, VA: Kimo Press, 1987.

Feinberg, David B. *Queer and Loathing: Rants and Raves of a Raging AIDS Clone*. New York: Viking, 1994.

Fine, Edith Hope. *Gary Paulsen: Author and Wilderness Adventurer*. Berkeley Heights, NJ: Enslow Publications, Inc., 2000.

Ford, Corey. *The Time of Laughter*. Boston, MA: Little, Brown and Company, 1967.

Ford, Michael Thomas. *Outspoken: Role Models from the Lesbian and Gay Community*. New York: Morrow Junior Books, 1998.

Freedman, Jeri. *Sid Fleischman*. New York: The Rosen Publishing Group, 2004.

Frist, Karyn McLaughlin, editor. *"Love you, Daddy Boy": Daughters Honor the Fathers They Love*. Lanham, MD: Taylor Trade Publishing, 2006.

Furst, Herbert. *The New Anecdotes of Painters and Paintings*. London: The Bodley Head, Ltd., 1926.

Gershick, Zsa Zsa. *Gay Old Girls*. Los Angeles, CA: Alyson Books, 1998.

Goodman, Jack, and Albert Rice. *I Wish I'd Said That!* New York: Simon and Schuster, 1935.

Greene, Meg. *Louis Sachar*. New York: The Rosen Publishing Group, 2004.

Grenfell, Joyce. *Joyce Grenfell Requests the Pleasure*. London: Macdonald Futura Publishers Ltd., 1976.

Heims, Neil. *J.R.R. Tolkien*. Philadelphia, PA: Chelsea House Publishers, 2004.

Henry, Lewis C. *Humorous Anecdotes About Famous People*. Garden City, NY: Halcyon House, 1948.

Hoekstra, Molly, editor. *Am I Teaching Yet? Stories from the Teacher-Training Trenches*. Portsmouth, NH: Heinemann, 2002.

Isenberg, Barbara. *State of the Arts: California Artists Talk About Their Work*. Chicago, IL: Ivan R. Dee, 2000.

Ishizuka, Kathy. *Asian American Authors*. Berkeley Heights, NJ: Enslow Publications, Inc., 2000.

Jones, Jen. *Judy Blume: Fearless Storyteller for Teens*. Berkeley Heights, NJ: Enslow Publishers, Inc., 2009.

Jordan, Denise M. *Walter Dean Myers: Writer for Real Teens*. Berkeley Heights, NJ: Enslow Publications, Inc., 1999.

Kehret, Peg. *Five Pages a Day: A Writer's Journey*. Morton Grove, IL: Albert Whitman & Company, 2002.

Kenan, Randall, and Amy Sickels. *James Baldwin*. Philadelphia, PA: Chelsea House Publishers, 2005.

Kovacs, Deborah. *Meet the Authors*. New York: Scholastic Professional Books, 1995.

Lee, Gwen, and Doris Elaine Sauter, editors. *What If Our World Is Their Heaven? The Final Conversations of Philip K. Dick*. Woodstock and New York: The Overlook Press, 2000.

Lee, Stan, and George Mair. *Excelsior! The Amazing Life of Stan Lee*. New York: Fireside, 2002.

Lennon, Adrian. *Jorge Luis Borges*. New York: Chelsea House Publishers, 1992.

Levin, Judy. *Christopher Paul Curtis*. New York: The Rosen Publishing Group, 2006.

Lewis, Mildred and Milton. *Famous Modern Newspaper Writers*. New York: Dodd, Mead & Company, 1962.

Liberman, Sherri. *Lynne Reid Banks*. New York: The Rosen Publishing Group, 2006.

Madison, Bob. *American Horror Writers*. Berkeley Heights, NJ: Enslow Publications, Inc., 2001.

Marcovitz, Hal. *R.L. Stine*. Philadelphia, PA: Chelsea House Publishers, 2006.

Marcus, Leonard S., compiler and editor. *Author Talk*. New York: Simon and Schuster Books for Young Readers, 2000.

Marcus, Leonard S., compiler and editor. *The Wand in the Word: Conversations with Writers of Fantasy*. Cambridge, MA: Candlewick Press, 2006.

Marinelli, Deborah A. *Virginia Hamilton*. New York: The Rosen Publishing Group, 2003.

McKee, Jenn. *Jack Kerouac*. Philadelphia, PA: Chelsea House Publishers, 2004.

McPhee, Nancy. *The Second Book of Insults*. Toronto, Canada: Van Nostrand Reinhold, Ltd., 1981.

Micklos, Jr., John. *Jerry Spinelli: Master Teller of Teen Tales*. Berkeley Heights, NJ: Enslow Publishers, Inc., 2008.

Miller, John, and Aaron Kenedi, editors. *Where Inspiration Lives: Writers, Artists, and Their Creative Places*. Novato, CA: New World Library, 2003.

Mullen, Tom. *Seriously, Life is a Laughing Matter*. Waco, TX: Word Books, 1978.

Otfinoski, Steven. *Stan Lee: Comic Book Genius*. New York: Franklin Watts, 2007.

Paulsen, Gary. *Guts: The True Stories Behind* Hatchet *and the Brian Books*. New York: Delacorte Press, 2001.

Pearson, Hesketh. *Lives of the Wits*. New York: Harper & Row, Publishers, 1962.

Rawding, F.W. *Gandhi and the Struggle for India's Independence*. Minneapolis, MN: Lerner Publications Company, 1982.

Reichard, Susan E. *Philip Pullman: Master of Fantasy*. Berkeley Heights, NJ: Enslow Publishers, Inc., 2006.

Restak, M.D., Richard. *Think Smart: A Neuroscientist's Prescription for Improving Your Brain's Performance*. New York: Riverhead Books, 2009.

Rollins, Charlemae. *Famous American Negro Poets*. New York: Dodd, Mead & Company, 1965.

Roman, Joseph. *Octavio Paz*. New York: Chelsea House Publishers, 1994.

Roman, Joseph. *Pablo Neruda*. New York: Chelsea House Publishers, 1992.

Rosenberg, Aaron. *Madeleine L'Engle*. New York: The Rosen Publishing Group, 2006.

Rutkowska, Wanda. *Famous People in Anecdotes*. Warszawa: Wydawnictwa Szkolne i Pedagogiczne, 1977.

Saidman, Anne. *Stephen King: Master of Horror*. Minneapolis, MN: Lerner Publications Company, 1992.

Shields, Charles J. *I am Scout: The Biography of Harper Lee*. New York: Henry Holt and Company, 2008.

Shields, Charles J. *Mythmaker: The Story of J.K. Rowling*. Philadelphia, PA: Chelsea House Publishers, 2002.

Silverthorne, Elizabeth. *Louisa May Alcott*. Philadelphia, PA: Chelsea House Publishers, 2002.

Singer, Marilyn. *Cats to the Rescue*. New York: Henry Holt and Company, 2006.

Sleator, William. *Oddballs*. New York: Dutton's Children's Books, 1993.

Smith, H. Allen. *The Compleat Practical Joker*. Garden City, NY: Doubleday and Company, Inc., 1953.

Sommers, Michael A. *Richard Peck*. New York: The Rosen Publishing Group, 2004.

Spring, Albert. *M.E. Kerr*. New York: The Rosen Publishing Group, 2006.

Steffens, Bradley. *J.K. Rowling*. San Diego, CA: Lucent Books, 2002.

Steinberg, Peter K. *Sylvia Plath*. Philadelphia, PA: Chelsea House Publishers, 2004.

Strickland, Michael R. *African-American Poets*. Springfield, NJ: Enslow Publications, Inc., 1996.

Telushkin, Rabbi Joseph. *Jewish Wisdom: Ethical, Spiritual, and Historical Lessons from the Great Works and Thinkers*. New York: William Morrow and Company, Inc., 1994.

Tevis, Jamie Griggs. *My Life with the Hustler*. Athens, OH: The Author, 2003.

Thompson, Anita. *The Gonzo Way: A Celebration of Hunter S. Thompson*. Golden, CO: Fulcrum Publishing, 2007.

Thomson, Sarah L. *Gary Paulsen*. New York: The Rosen Publishing Group, 2003.

Thomson, Sarah L. *Robert Cormier*. New York: The Rosen Publishing Group, 2003.

Tomedi, John. *Kurt Vonnegut*. Philadelphia, PA: Chelsea House Publishers, 2004.

Topol, Chaim, compiler. *Topol's Treasury of Jewish Humor, Wit and Wisdom*. New York: Barricade Books, Inc., 1994.

Wagner-Martin, Linda. *Barbara Kingsolver*. Philadelphia, PA: Chelsea House Publishers, 2004.

Weidt, Maryann N. *Oh, the Places He Went: A Story About Dr. Seuss*. Minneapolis, MN: Carolrhoda Books, Inc., 1994.

Willett, Edward. *Orson Scott Card: Architect of Alternate Worlds*. Berkeley Heights, NJ: Enslow Publishers, Inc., 2006.

Wilson, Antoine. *S.E. Hinton*. New York: The Rosen Publishing Group, 2003.

Wilson, Suzan. *Stephen King: King of Thrillers and Horror*. Berkeley Heights, NJ: Enslow Publications, Inc., 2000.

Woronov, Mary. *Swimming Underground: My Years in the Warhol Factory*. London: Serpent's Tail, 1995.

Yuan, Margaret Speaker. *Philip Pullman*. Philadelphia, PA: Chelsea House Publishers, 2006.

Appendix B: About the Author

It was a dark and stormy night. Suddenly a cry rang out, and on a hot summer night in 1954, Josephine, wife of Carl Bruce, gave birth to a boy — me. Unfortunately, this young married couple allowed Reuben Saturday, Josephine's brother, to name their first-born. Reuben, aka "The Joker," decided that Bruce was a nice name, so he decided to name me Bruce Bruce. I have gone by my middle name — David — ever since.

Being named Bruce David Bruce hasn't been all bad. Bank tellers remember me very quickly, so I don't often have to show an ID. It can be fun in charades, also. When I was a counselor as a teenager at Camp Echoing Hills in Warsaw, Ohio, a fellow counselor gave the signs for "sounds like" and "two words," then she pointed to a bruise on her leg twice. Bruise Bruise? Oh yeah, Bruce Bruce is the answer!

Uncle Reuben, by the way, gave me a haircut when I was in kindergarten. He cut my hair short and shaved a small bald spot on the back of my head. My mother wouldn't let me go to school until the bald spot grew out again.

Of all my brothers and sisters (six in all), I am the only transplant to Athens, Ohio. I was born in Newark, Ohio, and have lived all around Southeastern Ohio. However, I moved to Athens to go to Ohio University and have never left.

At Ohio U, I never could make up my mind whether to major in English or Philosophy, so I got a bachelor's degree with a double major in both areas, then I added a Master of Arts degree in English and a Master of Arts degree in Philosophy. Yes, I have my MAMA degree.

Currently, and for a long time to come (I eat fruits and veggies), I am spending my retirement writing books such as *Nadia Comaneci: Perfect 10*, *The Funniest People in Comedy*, *Homer's* Iliad: *A Retelling in Prose*, and *William Shakespeare's* Hamlet: *A Retelling in Prose*.

If all goes well, I will publish one or two books a year for the rest of my life. (On the other hand, a good way to make God laugh is to tell Her your plans.)

By the way, my sister Brenda Kennedy writes romances such as *A New Beginning* and *Shattered Dreams*.

Appendix C: Some Books by David Bruce

Anecdote Collections

250 Anecdotes About Opera
250 Anecdotes About Religion
250 Anecdotes About Religion: Volume 2
250 Music Anecdotes
Be a Work of Art: 250 Anecdotes and Stories
The Coolest People in Art: 250 Anecdotes
The Coolest People in the Arts: 250 Anecdotes
The Coolest People in Books: 250 Anecdotes
The Coolest People in Comedy: 250 Anecdotes
Create, Then Take a Break: 250 Anecdotes
Don't Fear the Reaper: 250 Anecdotes
The Funniest People in Art: 250 Anecdotes
The Funniest People in Books: 250 Anecdotes
The Funniest People in Books, Volume 2: 250 Anecdotes
The Funniest People in Books, Volume 3: 250 Anecdotes
The Funniest People in Comedy: 250 Anecdotes
The Funniest People in Dance: 250 Anecdotes
The Funniest People in Families: 250 Anecdotes
The Funniest People in Families, Volume 2: 250 Anecdotes
The Funniest People in Families, Volume 3: 250 Anecdotes
The Funniest People in Families, Volume 4: 250 Anecdotes
The Funniest People in Families, Volume 5: 250 Anecdotes
The Funniest People in Families, Volume 6: 250 Anecdotes
The Funniest People in Movies: 250 Anecdotes
The Funniest People in Music: 250 Anecdotes
The Funniest People in Music, Volume 2: 250 Anecdotes
The Funniest People in Music, Volume 3: 250 Anecdotes
The Funniest People in Neighborhoods: 250 Anecdotes
The Funniest People in Relationships: 250 Anecdotes
The Funniest People in Sports: 250 Anecdotes
The Funniest People in Sports, Volume 2: 250 Anecdotes
The Funniest People in Television and Radio: 250 Anecdotes
The Funniest People in Theater: 250 Anecdotes

The Funniest People Who Live Life: 250 Anecdotes
The Funniest People Who Live Life, Volume 2: 250 Anecdotes
The Kindest People Who Do Good Deeds, Volume 1: 250 Anecdotes
The Kindest People Who Do Good Deeds, Volume 2: 250 Anecdotes
Maximum Cool: 250 Anecdotes
The Most Interesting People in Movies: 250 Anecdotes
The Most Interesting People in Politics and History: 250 Anecdotes
The Most Interesting People in Politics and History, Volume 2: 250 Anecdotes
The Most Interesting People in Politics and History, Volume 3: 250 Anecdotes
The Most Interesting People in Religion: 250 Anecdotes
The Most Interesting People in Sports: 250 Anecdotes
The Most Interesting People Who Live Life: 250 Anecdotes
The Most Interesting People Who Live Life, Volume 2: 250 Anecdotes
Reality is Fabulous: 250 Anecdotes and Stories
Resist Psychic Death: 250 Anecdotes
Seize the Day: 250 Anecdotes and Stories

[1] Source: Roger Ebert, "Paul Galloway: A beloved legend." *Chicago Sun-Times.* 3 February 2009 <http://rogerebert.suntimes.com/apps/pbcs.dll/article?AID=/20090203/PEOPLE/902039997>.

[2] Source: Robert McCrum, "A thriller in ten chapters." *The Guardian.* 25 May 2008 <http://books.guardian.co.uk/departments/generalfiction/story/0,,2282065,00.html>.

[3] Source: Suzan Wilson, *Stephen King: King of Thrillers and Horror*, p. 67.

[4] Source: Gary Paulsen, *Guts: The True Stories Behind Hatchet and the Brian Books*, p. 102.

[5] Source: John Micklos, Jr., *Jerry Spinelli: Master Teller of Teen Tales*, p. 68.

[6] Source: Marilyn Singer, *Cats to the Rescue*, p. 102.

[7] Source: Lulu.com. 1 April 2010 <http://www.lulu.com/>.

[8] Source: Susanna Daniel, *Karen Cushman*, pp. 14-15, 20-24, 80.

[9] Source: Susan E. Reichard, *Philip Pullman: Master of Fantasy*, pp. 11, 19, 82.

[10] Source: Sarah L. Thomson, *Robert Cormier*, pp. 7, 39-40, 59.

[11] Source: Antoine Wilson, *S.E. Hinton*, pp. 7-9, 81.

[12] Source: Jamie Griggs Tevis, *My Life with the Hustler*, p. 246.

[13] Source: Donald Fagen, "The Man Who Told A Christmas Story." *Slate.* 22 December 2008 <http://www.slate.com/id/2207058/pagenum/all/#p2>.

[14] Source: Paul Collins, "; (: Has Modern Life Killed the Semicolon?" Slate. 20 June 2008 <http://www.slate.com/id/2194087/>.

[15] Source: Lawrence J. Epstein, *A Treasury of Jewish Anecdotes*, p. 12.

[16] Source: Gwen Lee and Doris Elaine Sauter, eds. *What If Our World Is Their Heaven? The Final Conversations of Philip K. Dick*, p. 17.

[17] Source: Molly Hoekstra, editor, *Am I Teaching Yet?*, p. 47.

[18] Source: Bradley Steffens, *J.K. Rowling*, pp. 48-49, 59.

[19] Source: Jeri Freedman, *Sid Fleischman*, pp. 35-37, 40.

[20] Source: Nathaniel Benchley, *Robert Benchley*, p. 189.

[21] Source: Corey Ford, *The Time of Laughter*, p. 100.

[22] Source: William Compson, *J.K. Rowling*, p. 52.

[23] Source: Everett S. Allen, *Famous American Humorous Poets*, p. 94.

[24] Source: Allen Pierleoni, "Back from the future: Robert Silverberg has guided sci-fi readers for 55 years." 25 June 2008 <http://www.popmatters.com/pm/news/article/60177/back-from-the-future-robert-silverberg-has-guided-sci-fi-readers-for-55-yea/>.

[25] Source: Paul Constant, "Text Message from Los Angeles." *The Stranger*. 18 June 2008 <http://www.thestranger.com/seattle/Content?oid=601461>.

[26] Source: Connie Ogle, "A non-Western guy's great Western." McClatchy Newspapers. 4 June 2008 http://www.popmatters.com/pm/news/article/59402/a-non-western-guys-great-western/.

[27] Source: William Donaldson, *Great Disasters of the Stage*, p. 33.

[28] Source: Sarah L. Thomson, *Gary Paulsen*, pp. 31-32, 73.

[29] Source: Paulo Coelho, *Confessions of a Pilgrim*, p. 166.

[30] Source: Carol Dommermuth-Costa, *Agatha Christie: Writer of Mystery*, pp. 90-91.

[31] Source: Barbara Kingsolver, "Your Money or Your Life." Humanity.org. 11 May 2008 <http://humanity.org/voices/commencements/speeches/index.php?page=kingsolver_at_duke>. This is Ms. Kingsolver's commencement address that she gave 11 May 2008 at Duke University in Durham, North Carolina.

[32] Source: John Hind, "Kathy Lette." *The Guardian*. 20 December 2009 <http://www.guardian.co.uk/lifeandstyle/2009/dec/20/kathy-lette-in-her-own-words>. Also: Kathy Lette, "Quiplash." Accessed 21 December 2009 <http://www.kathylette.com/quiplash.htm>.

[33] Source: John Carey, "George Orwell's son speaks out about his father." *The Times*. 15 March 2009 <http://entertainment.timesonline.co.uk/tol/arts_and_entertainment/books/non-fiction/article5889541.ece>.

[34] Source: Nzingha Clarke, *Karen Hesse*, pp. 13-16.

[35] Source: Neil Heims, *J.R.R. Tolkien*, p. 66.

[36] Source: Nancy Crampton, photographer, *Writers*, pp. 58-59.

[37] Source: Barbara Isenberg, *State of the Arts: California Artists Talk About Their Work*, pp. 111-112.

[38] Source: Carmen Bredeson, *American Writers of the 20th Century*, p. 19.

[39] Source: Tom Mullen, *Seriously, Life is a Laughing Matter*, p. 32.

[40]Source: Herbert Furst, *The New Anecdotes of Painters and Paintings*, p. 55.

[41]Source: Edith Hope Fine, *Gary Paulsen: Author and Wilderness Adventurer*, p. 109.

[42] Source: James Campbell, "Voice of the people." *The Guardian*. 24 May 2008 <http://books.guardian.co.uk/review/story/0,,2281913,00.html>.

[43] Source: Bryan Appleyard: "Hazzard: greatest novelist of 20th century?" *The Sunday Times*. 18 May 2008 <http://entertainment.timesonline.co.uk/tol/arts_and_entertainment/books/article3933418.ece>.

[44] Source: William Rodney Allen, editor, *Conversations with Kurt Vonnegut*, p. 299.

[45] Source: John Tomedi, *Kurt Vonnegut*, pp. 119, 128.

[46] Source: Nikki Tranter, "Laughing With Them: An Interview with GoFugYourself Creators Jessica Morgan and Heather Cocks." 22 May 2008 <http://www.popmatters.com/pm/blogs/reprint_post/58963/laughing-with-them-an-interview-with-gofugyourself-creators-jessica-morgan->. You can see their blog at <http://gofugyourself.typepad.com/>.

[47]Source: Rabbi Joseph Telushkin, *Jewish Wisdom*, pp. 189-190.

[48] Source: William Rodney Allen, editor, *Conversations with Kurt Vonnegut*, p. 166.

[49]Source: Cyril Clemens, "An Evening with A.E. Housman," p. 10.

[50] Source: Victor Bockris, *With William Burroughs: A Report from the Bunker*, pp. 41-42, 156.

[51] Source: Rick Kogan, "Studs Terkel dies." *Chicago Tribune*. 31 October 2008 <http://www.chicagotribune.com/news/local/chi-studs-terkel-dead,0,3592218,full.story>.

[52] Source: Nzingha Clarke, *Karen Hesse*, p. 29.

[53] Source: Cynthia Ozick, "Writers, Visible and Invisible." *Standpoint*. September 2008 <http://www.standpointmag.co.uk./node/390/full>.

[54]Source: Nathaniel Benchley, *Robert Benchley*, pp. 10-11.

[55]Source: Lewis C. Henry, *Humorous Anecdotes About Famous People*, p. 44.

[56] Source: Daniel Zalewski, " THE BACKGROUND HUM: Ian McEwan's art of unease." *The New Yorker*. 23 February 2009 <http://www.newyorker.com/

reporting/2009/02/23/090223fa_fact_zalewski?currentPage=all>. Also: Katie Nicholl, "Novelist Ian McEwan's son didn't make the grade." *Daily Mail.* 20 October 2007 <http://www.dailymail.co.uk/tvshowbiz/article-488781/Novelist-Ian-McEwans-son-didnt-make-grade.html>.

[57] Source: Karen Burshtein, *Walter Dean Myers*, pp. 26-30.

[58] Source: Anita Thompson, *The Gonzo Way: A Celebration of Hunter S. Thompson*, pp. 23-26.

[59] Source: Kimberly Campbell, *Richard Peck: A Spellbinding Storyteller*, pp. 38-39, 79.

[60] Source: Michael R. Strickland, *African-American Poets*, pp. 55-58.

[61] Source: Elizabeth Silverthorne, *Louisa May Alcott*, p. 19.

[62] Source: Wanda Rutkowska, *Famous People in Anecdotes*, p. 18.

[63] Source: Susanna Daniel, *Jane Yolen*, pp. 8-9, 16, 24.

[64] Source: Michael A. Sommers, *Richard Peck*, p. 21.

[65] Source: William Sleator, *Oddballs*, p. 63.

[66] Source: Christopher Benfey, "Review of *Flannery: A Life of Flannery O'Connor* by Brad Gooch." 28 May 2009 <http://www.powells.com/review/2009_05_28.html>.

[67] Source: Rabbi Joseph Telushkin, *Jewish Wisdom*, p. 202.

[68] Source: Sherri Liberman, *Lynne Reid Banks*, p. 38.

[69] Source: Albert Spring, *M.E. Kerr*, pp. 31, 70.

[70] Source: Lewis C. Henry, *Humorous Anecdotes About Famous People*, p. 126.

[71] Source: Jonathan Derbyshire, "An American suicide." *New Statesman.* 27 November 2008 <http://www.newstatesman.com/books/2008/11/wallace-fiction-mccain>.

[72] Source: Charlemae Rollins, *Famous American Negro Poets*, p. 77.

[73] Source: Emma Brockes, "Letters from my father." *The Guardian.* 27 September 2008 <http://www.guardian.co.uk/culture/2008/sep/27/radio.radio>.

[74] Source: Dana Goodyear, "Kid Goth: Neil Gaiman's Fantasies." *The New Yorker.* 25 January 2010 <http://www.newyorker.com/reporting/2010/01/25/100125fa_fact_goodyear?currentPage=all>.

[75] Source: Sean Dolin, *Gabriel García Marquez*, p. 25.

[76] Source: "*Cheever: A Life*, by Blake Bailey": A review by Jonathan Dee. 12 March 2010 <http://www.powells.com/review/2010_03_12.html>. This review appeared originally in *Harper's Magazine*.

[77]Source: Hesketh Pearson, *Lives of the Wits*, p. 292.

[78] Source: Jayme Lynn Blaschke, *Voices of Vision: Creators of Science Fiction and Fantasy Speak*, pp. 168-169.

[79] Source: John Miller and Aaron Kenedi, editors, *Where Inspiration Lives: Writers, Artists, and Their Creative Places*, p. 71.

[80] Source: Michael Gray Baughan, *Charles Bukowski*, pp. 21, 31-32, 43, 45, 66, 77.

[81] Source: Richard Restak, M.D., *Think Smart: A Neuroscientist's Prescription for Improving Your Brain's Performance*, p. 128.

[82] Source: John Tomedi, *Kurt Vonnegut*, p. 132.

[83] Source: David Carter, *George Santayana*, p. 26.

[84] Source: Margaret Speaker Yuan, *Philip Pullman*, pp. 53-54.

[85] Source: Aida Edemariam, "Alexandra Shulman interview: Keep chic and carry on." *The Guardian*. 5 December 2009 <http://www.guardian.co.uk/theguardian/2009/dec/05/alexandra-shulman-interview>.

[86]Source: Gary Paulsen, *Guts: The True Stories Behind* Hatchet *and the Brian Books*, pp. 123-124.

[87] Source: Jen Jones, *Judy Blume: Fearless Storyteller for Teens*, p. 44.

[88] Source: Peter K. Steinberg, *Sylvia Plath*, p. 55.

[89]Source: Nancy McPhee, *The Second Book of Insults*, p. 18.

[90]Source: Jerry Clower, *Stories from Home*, p. 23.

[91] Source: David Carter, *George Santayana*, p. 68.

[92]Source: F.W. Rawding, *Gandhi and the Struggle for India's Independence*, p. 27.

[93] Source: Jen Jones, *Judy Blume: Fearless Storyteller for Teens*, pp. 41, 51.

[94]Source: Michael Thomas Ford, *Outspoken*, p. 55.

[95]Source: Chuck Fager, *Quakers are Funny!*, p. 65.

[96] Source: Anne Lamott, "20 Questions." Popmatters.com. 5 April 2010 <http://www.popmatters.com/pm/feature/123402-anne-lamott/>.

[97] Source: Anita Thompson, *The Gonzo Way: A Celebration of Hunter S. Thompson*, pp. 27-28.

[98] Source: Joseph Roman, *Pablo Neruda*, p. 62.

[99] Source: Susan Dominus, "Suze Orman Is Having a Moment." *The New York Times Magazine.* <http://www.nytimes.com/2009/05/17/magazine/17orman-t.html?pagewanted=4&_r=2&hp>.

[100] Source: Michael Thomas Ford, *Outspoken*, pp. 21-22.

[101] Source: Zsa Zsa Gershick, *Gay Old Girls*, p. 36.

[102] Source: Lesléa Newman, "Introduction" to Randall Kenan and Amy Sickels' *James Baldwin*, p. xv.

[103] Source: Paul Bailey, editor, *The Stately Homo: A Celebration of the Life of Quentin Crisp*, p. 40.

[104] Source: Garry Wills, "Daredevil." *The Atlantic.* July/August 2009 <http://www.theatlantic.com/doc/200907/william-buckley>.

[105] Source: Elizabeth Silverthorne, *Louisa May Alcott*, pp. 26-27.

[106] Source: Danielle Crittenden, "The Reno: How A Minor Repair Gutted My Kitchen." 11 July 2008. Huffington Post. <http://www.huffingtonpost.com/danielle-crittenden/the-reno-my-silk-robe-was_b_112152.html>.

[107] Source: Joyce Grenfell, *Joyce Grenfell Requests the Pleasure*, p. 161.

[108] Source: Sarah L. Thomson, *Robert Cormier*, pp. 25, 47, 74-75.

[109] Source: Virginia Brackett, *Restless Genius: The Story of Virginia Woolf*, pp. 99-100.

[110] Source: Charles J. Shields, *I am Scout: The Biography of Harper Lee*, pp. 1-2.

[111] Source: Bradley Steffens, *J.K. Rowling*, pp. 28-29, 44-45.

[112] Source: Randall Kenan and Amy Sickels, *James Baldwin*, pp. 66-67.

[113] Source: Tanya Dean, *Theodor Geisel (Dr. Seuss)*, pp. 96-97.

[114] Source: Judy Levin, *Christopher Paul Curtis*, pp. 15-16.

[115] Source: Antoine Wilson, *S.E. Hinton*, pp. 30-32, 39, 72-73, 79-80..

[116] Source: Judy Levin, *Christopher Paul Curtis*, pp. 52-53.

[117] Source: Meg Greene, *Louis Sachar*, p. 29.

[118] Source: Scott Timberg, "Philip K. Dick: A 'plastic' paradox." *Los Angeles Times*. 24 January 2010 <http://www.latimes.com/entertainment/news/arts/la-ca-philip-k-dick24-2010jan24,0,2001774,full.story>.

[119] Source: Anne Saidman, *Stephen King: Master of Horror*, pp. 16, 31.

[120] Source: Aaron Rosenberg, *Madeleine L'Engle*, p. 78.

[121] Source: Paul Arendt, Anita Sethi and Dave Simpson, interviewers. "'If that goes off again I'll kill you.'" *The Guardian*. 11 September 2008 <http://www.guardian.co.uk/stage/2008/sep/11/comedy>.

[122] Source: Chaim Topol, compiler, *Topol's Treasury of Jewish Humor, Wit and Wisdom*, p. 101.

[123] Source: Simon Barnes, "The genius of Dick Francis was to give readers a racing certainty." *The Times*. 15 February 2010 <http://entertainment.timesonline.co.uk/tol/arts_and_entertainment/books/article7027046.ece>.

[124] Source: David B. Feinberg, *Queer and Loathing: Rants and Raves of a Raging AIDS Clone*, p. 135.

[125] Source: Jack Goodman and Albert Rice, *I Wish I'd Said That!*, pp. 98-99.

[126] Source: Nancy McPhee, *The Second Book of Insults*, p. 16.

[127] Source: Robert S. McElvaine, "George Carlin: An Irish Mensch." Huffingtonpost.com. 23 June 2008 <http://www.huffingtonpost.com/robert-s-mcelvaine/george-carlin-an-irish-me_b_108797.html>.

[128] Source: Ian McEwan, "Ian McEwan on language and inheritance." *The Times*. 15 March 2009 <http://entertainment.timesonline.co.uk/tol/arts_and_entertainment/books/book_reviews/article5889765.ece>.

[129] Source: Zsa Zsa Gershick, *Gay Old Girls*, p. 191.

[130] Source: Hesketh Pearson, *Lives of the Wits*, p. 102.

[131] Source: Herbert Furst, *The New Anecdotes of Painters and Paintings*, pp. 66-67.

[132] Source: Owen Vaughan, "Mr Marvel: the secret origin of Stan Lee." *The Times*. 30 January 2009 <http://entertainment.timesonline.co.uk/tol/arts_and_entertainment/film/article6892312.ece>.

[133] Source: Aaron Rosenberg, *Madeleine L'Engle*, pp. 42-45.

[134] Source: Patricia Cornwell, "20 Questions." Popmatters. 19 October 2009 <http://www.popmatters.com/pm/feature/112941-patricia-cornwell/>.

[135] Source: Carol Dommermuth-Costa, *Emily Dickinson: Singular Poet*, p. 44.

[136] Source: John Micklos, Jr., *Jerry Spinelli: Master Teller of Teen Tales*, pp. 24-25.

[137] Source: Michael A. Sommers, *Richard Peck*, pp. 55, 72-73.

[138] Source: Karyn McLaughlin Frist, editor, *"Love you, Daddy Boy": Daughters Honor the Fathers They Love*, pp. xii, 83.

[139] Source: Albert Spring, *M.E. Kerr*, p. 20.

[140] Source: Douglas Biggers, "The story of a little newspaper, now 25 years old, that almost didn't make it." *Tucson Weekly*. 26 February 2009 <http://www.tucsonweekly.com/gbase/Opinion/Content?oid=oid:122510>.

[141] Source: Tom Danehy, "Looking back on more than two decades of colleagues and hate mail." *Tucson Weekly*. 26 February 2009 <http://www.tucsonweekly.com/gbase/Opinion/Content?oid=oid:122506>.

[142] Source: Jack Goodman and Albert Rice, *I Wish I'd Said That!*, pp. 124-125.

[143] Source: Pete Paphides, "Paul McCartney's smokescreen." *The Times*. 19 December 2008 <http://entertainment.timesonline.co.uk/tol/arts_and_entertainment/music/article5365557.ece>.

[144] Source: Chuck Fager, *Quakers are Funny!*, p. 63.

[145] Source: Gary Younge, "Maya Angelou: "I'm fine as wine in the summertime.' *The Guardian*. 14 November 2009 <http://www.guardian.co.uk/books/2009/nov/14/maya-angelou-interview>.

[146] Source: Hal Marcovitz, *R.L. Stine*, p. 27.

[147] Source: Terry Jones, "Terry Jones remembers Douglas Adams, 'the last of the Pythons.'" Timesonline.co.uk. 10 October 2009 <http://entertainment.timesonline.co.uk/tol/arts_and_entertainment/tv_and_radio/article6866840.ece>.

[148] Source: Leslie Goldman, "How Ugly People Succeed." Theweightinggame.ivillage.com. 30 June 2008 <http://theweightinggame.ivillage.com/dietfitness/2008/06/calling_all_ugly_1.html>.

[149] Source: Geoffrey Wheatcroft, "Bondage." *New York Review of Books*. Volume 55, Number 13. 14 August 2008 <http://www.nybooks.com/articles/21712>.

[150] Source: Paulo Coelho, *Confessions of a Pilgrim*, pp. x-xi, 111-112.

[151] Source: Rosanna Greenstreet, "Q&A with Zoë Heller, novelist." *The Guardian*. 8 November 2008 <http://www.guardian.co.uk/lifeandstyle/2008/nov/08/zoe-heller>.

[152] Source: Steve Paul, "Tony Hillerman revealed the riches of Navajo life to outsiders." McClatchy Newspapers. 5 November 2008 <http://www.popmatters.com/pm/article/65355/tony-hillerman-revealed-the-riches-of-navajo-life-to-outsiders/>.

[153] Source: Joyce Grenfell, *Joyce Grenfell Requests the Pleasure*, p. 110.

[154] Source: Virginia Brackett, *Restless Genius: The Story of Virginia Woolf*, p. 17.

[155] Source: Edith Hope Fine, *Gary Paulsen: Author and Wilderness Adventurer*, p. 61.

[156] Source: Lisa Rondinelli Albert, *Lois Lowry: The Giver of Stories and Memories*, pp. 57, 106.

[157] Source: Michael Bedard, *William Blake: The Gates of Paradise*, pp. 11, 136, 165.

[158] Source: Michael Greenberg, "Review of *Gabriel García Márquez: A Life* by Gerald Martin." *New York Review of Books*. Volume 56, Number 12. 16 July 2009 <http://www.nybooks.com/articles/22892>.

[159] Source: Stan Lee and George Mair, *Excelsior! The Amazing Life of Stan Lee*, pp. 214-216.

[160] Source: Sandra Brown, "20 Questions." Popmatters.com. 24 November 2009 <http://www.popmatters.com/pm/feature/116643-sandra-brown/>.

[161] Source: John Bogle, "Keep Investing." *Rational Angle*. 5 October 2008 <http://rationalangle.blogspot.com/2008/10/john-bogle-keep-investing.html>.

[162] Source: William Sleator, *Oddballs*, pp. 64-65.

[163] Source: Carmen Bredeson, *American Writers of the 20th Century*, p. 69.

[164] Source: Linda Wagner-Martin, *Barbara Kingsolver*, p. 48.

[165] Source: Charles J. Shields, *Mythmaker: The Story of J.K. Rowling*, pp. 19, 23, 47.

[166] Source: Mary Woronov, *Swimming Underground: My Years in the Warhol Factory*, pp. 50, 141.

[167] Source: Carmen Bredeson, *American Writers of the 20th Century*, pp. 78-79.

[168] Source: Linda Wagner-Martin, *Barbara Kingsolver*, pp. 6, 8.

[169] Source: Emma Brockes, "The queen of the digital water cooler." *The Guardian*. 10 October 2009 <http://www.guardian.co.uk/media/2009/oct/10/arianna-huffington-interview>.

[170] Source: Steven Otfinoski, *Stan Lee: Comic Book Genius*, pp. 7, 12-13, 19.

[171] Source: Charles J. Shields, *Mythmaker: The Story of J.K. Rowling*, p. 42.

[172] Source: Charlemae Rollins, *Famous American Negro Poets*, pp. 57-58.

[173] Source: Sarah L. Thomson, *Gary Paulsen*, p. 26.

[174] Source: Carol Bauer Church, *Carol Burnett: Star of Comedy*, p. 5.

[175] Source: Jonathan Raban, "The Prodigious Pessimist." 8 December 2008 <http://www.powells.com/review/2008_12_08.html>. This review originally appeared in the *New York Review of Books*.

[176] Source: Jayme Lynn Blaschke, *Voices of Vision: Creators of Science Fiction and Fantasy Speak*, pp. 31, 99-100.

[177] Source: Maryann N. Weidt, *Oh, the Places He Went: A Story About Dr. Seuss*, pp. 15-16, 24.

[178] Source: Edward Willett, *Orson Scott Card: Architect of Alternate Worlds*, pp. 16, 58.

[179] Source: Steven G. Kellman, "The scourge of the Lege." *San Antonio Current*. 21 October 2009 <http://sacurrent.com/arts/story.asp?id=70608>.

[180] Source: "*George, Being George: George Plimpton's Life as Told, Admired, Deplored, and Envied by 200 Friends, Relatives, Lovers, Acquaintances, Rivals*, by Nelson W. Aldrich: A review by Scott Sherman." *The Nation*. 15 January 2009 <http://www.thenation.com/doc/20090202/sherman/>.

[181] Source: Bob Madison, *American Horror Writers*, pp. 17, 21.

[182] Source: Michael R. Strickland, *African-American Poets*, p. 8.

[183] Source: Joseph Roman, *Octavio Paz*, p. 30.

[184] Source: Joseph Roman, *Pablo Neruda*, p. 36.

[185] Source: Chaim Topol, compiler, *Topol's Treasury of Jewish Humor, Wit and Wisdom*, p. 126.

[186] Source: Sean Dolin, *Gabriel García Marquez*, pp. 114-115.

[187] Source: Victor Bockris, *With William Burroughs: A Report from the Bunker*, p. 14.

[188] Source: Tanya Dean, *Theodor Geisel (Dr. Seuss)*, pp. 94-95.

[189] Source: Nancy Crampton, photographer, *Writers*, pp. 28-29.

[190] Source: Lawrence J. Epstein, *A Treasury of Jewish Anecdotes*, p. 215.

[191] Source: Benjamin Ivry, "No Panthéon for Camus." *New Statesman*. 17 December 2009 <http://www.newstatesman.com/books/2009/12/albert-camus-sarkozy-french>.

[192] Source: Adrian Lennon, *Jorge Luis Borges*, pp. 79-80.

[193] Source: Nick Mamatas, "The Term Paper Artist." *The Smart Set*. 10 October 2008 <http://www.thesmartset.com:80/article/article10100801.aspx>.

[194] Source: H. Allen Smith, *The Compleat Practical Joker*, pp. 8-9.

[195] Source: Neil Heims, *J.R.R. Tolkien*, pp. 27-28.

[196] Source: H. Allen Smith, *The Compleat Practical Joker*, pp. 194-195.

[197] Source: Maryann N. Weidt, *Oh, the Places He Went: A Story About Dr. Seuss*, p. 50.

[198] Source: Deborah A. Marinelli, *Virginia Hamilton*, pp. 20, 23-24.

[199] Source: Michael Billington, "Tennessee Williams: the quiet revolutionary." *The Guardian*. 27 July 2009 <http://www.guardian.co.uk/stage/2009/jul/27/tennessee-williams>.

[200] Source: Adrian Lennon, *Jorge Luis Borges*, p. 48.

[201] Source: Leonard S. Marcus, compiler and editor, *The Wand in the Word: Conversations with Writers of Fantasy*, pp. 157-59.

[202] Source: Gary Younge, "Andrea Levy: 'I started to realise what fiction could be. And I thought, wow! You can take on the world.'" *The Guardian*. 30 January 2010 <http://www.guardian.co.uk/books/2010/jan/30/andrea-levy-long-song-interview>.

[203] Source: Steven Otfinoski, *Stan Lee: Comic Book Genius*, p. 46.

[204]Source: Carol Dommermuth-Costa, *Agatha Christie: Writer of Mystery*, pp. 81-82.

[205] Source: Peg Kehret, *Five Pages a Day: A Writer's Journey*, pp. 44-45.

[206]Source: Suzan Wilson, *Stephen King: King of Thrillers and Horror*, p. 38.

[207]Source: Anne Saidman, *Stephen King: Master of Horror*, p. 41.

[208] Source: Leonard S. Marcus, compiler and editor, *The Wand in the Word: Conversations with Writers of Fantasy*, p. 138.

[209] Source: Charles J. Shields, *I am Scout: The Biography of Harper Lee*, p. 79.

[210]Source: Jamie Griggs Tevis, *My Life with the Hustler*, p. 221.

[211] Source: Karen Burshtein, *Walter Dean Myers*, pp. 41-42, 74-75.

[212] Source: Roger Ebert, "The best damn job in the whole damn world." 3 April 2009 <http://blogs.suntimes.com/ebert/2009/04/the_best_job_in_the_world.html>.

[213]Source: Wanda Rutkowska, *Famous People in Anecdotes*, pp. 26-27.

[214]Source: Peg Bracken, *But I Wouldn't Have Missed It for the World!*, p. 177.

[215]Source: Corey Ford, *The Time of Laughter*, p. 131.

[216] Source: Ed Caesar, "Don DeLillo: A writer like no other." *Sunday Times*. 21 February 2010 <http://entertainment.timesonline.co.uk/tol/arts_and_entertainment/books/article7031290.ece>.

[217] Source: Margaret Speaker Yuan, *Philip Pullman*, pp. 16-17.

[218] Source: John Miller and Aaron Kenedi, editors, *Where Inspiration Lives: Writers, Artists, and Their Creative Places*, p. 37.

[219]Source: Deborah Kovacs, *Meet the Authors*, p. 107.

[220]Source: Leonard S. Marcus, compiler and editor, *Author Talk*, p. 22.

[221] Source: Peg Kehret, *Five Pages a Day: A Writer's Journey*, p. 160.

[222] Source: Tom Danehy, "Tom has queries about eegee's ranch dressing, people who take up two parking spaces and Björk." *Tucson Weekly*. 27 November 2008 <http://www.tucsonweekly.com/gbase/Opinion/Content?oid=oid:118997>.

[223] Source: Jenn McKee, *Jack Kerouac*, pp. 42-43.

[224]Source: Paul Bailey, editor, *The Stately Homo: A Celebration of the Life of Quentin Crisp*, pp. 20-21.

[225] Source: Karyn McLaughlin Frist, editor, *"Love you, Daddy Boy": Daughters Honor the Fathers They Love*, p. 112.

[226] Source: Marc Ramirez, "Fans of popular vampire series pumping new blood into Forks, Wash." *The Seattle Times*. 30 July 2008 <http://www.popmatters.com/pm/article/61539/fans-of-popular-vampire-series-pumping-new-blood-into-forks-wash/>.

[227] Source: Joshua Kendall, "Noah Webster: The definition of Yankee know-how." *Los Angeles Times*. 15 October 2008 <http://www.latimes.com/news/opinion/commentary/la-oe-kendall15-2008oct15,0,596880.story>.

[228] Source: Peg Bracken, *But I Wouldn't Have Missed It for the World!*, p. 30.

[229] Source: Neil Hallows, "Why typewriters beat computers." BBC. 30 May 2008 <http://news.bbc.co.uk/1/hi/magazine/7427237.stm>.

[230] Source: Lisa Rondinelli Albert, *Lois Lowry: The Giver of Stories and Memories*, pp. 58-60.

[231] Source: Carol Dommermuth-Costa, *Emily Dickinson: Singular Poet*, p. 37.

[232] Source: Kathy Ishizuka, *Asian American Authors*, pp. 89-90, 93-94.

[233] Source: Jonathan Yardley, "The Memoirs of a Film Critic Par Excellence." Powells.com. 13 February 2009 <http://www.powells.com/review/2009_02_13.html>. This article appeared originally in the *Washington Post*. The anecdote appeared in Mr. Thomson's book titled *Try to Tell the Story: A Memoir*, of which this article is a review.

[234] Source: Cyril Clemens, "An Evening with A.E. Housman," pp. 12-13.

[235] Source: Adam Sage, "Anna Sam's book skewers shoppers." *The Times*. 7 June 2008 <http://entertainment.timesonline.co.uk/tol/arts_and_entertainment/books/article4083358.ece>.

[236] Source: Barbara Isenberg, *State of the Arts: California Artists Talk About Their Work*, pp. 60, 62.

[237] Source: Rachel Leibrock, "For Daniel Handler, Snicket lives — as do music and flying saucers." McClatchy Newspapers. 4 February 2009 <http://www.popmatters.com/pm/article/69987-for-daniel-handler-snicket-lives-as-do-music-and-flying-saucers/>.

[238] Source: Kimberly Campbell, *Richard Peck: A Spellbinding Storyteller*, pp. 28-29.

[239] Source: Edmund White, "The Strange Charms of John Cheever." *New York Review of Books*. Volume 57, Number 6, 8 April 2010 <http://www.nybooks.com/articles/23772>.

[240] Source: Susanna Daniel, *Jane Yolen*, pp. 62-63, 70.

[241] Source: Chris Vognar, "Dennis Lehane, a favorite author with filmmakers, expands his literary horizon." *The Dallas Morning News*. 16 July 2008 <http://www.popmatters.com/pm/article/61014/dennis-lehane-a-favorite-author-with-filmmakers-expands-his-literary-horizo/>.

[242]Source: Stan Lee and George Mair, *Excelsior! The Amazing Life of Stan Lee*, pp. 137-138.

[243]Source: Denise M. Jordan, *Walter Dean Myers: Writer for Real Teens*, pp. 105-107.

[244]Source: Bob Madison, *American Horror Writers*, pp. 35, 40.

[245] Source: Peter K. Steinberg, *Sylvia Plath*, p. 6. This anecdote is recounted in Linda Wagner-Martin's "Introduction" to this biography.

[246]Source: Leonard S. Marcus, compiler and editor, *Author Talk*, pp. 44-45.

[247]Source: Everett S. Allen, *Famous American Humorous Poets*, p. 51.

[248] Source: Julia Keller, "Inside the world of Neil Gaiman: 'Coraline' author living his dream life." *Chicago Tribune*. 27 May 2009 <http://www.popmatters.com/pm/article/93991-inside-the-world-of-neil-gaiman-coraline-author-living-his-dream-life/>.

[249]Source: Kathy Ishizuka, *Asian American Authors*, p. 83.

[250]Source: Mildred and Milton Lewis, *Famous Modern Newspaper Writers*, p. 67.